THE
PINKS

THE
PINKS

THE FIRST WOMEN DETECTIVES, OPERATIVES, AND
SPIES WITH THE PINKERTON NATIONAL DETECTIVE AGENCY

CHRIS ENSS

TWODOT®

GUILFORD, CONNECTICUT
HELENA, MONTANA

Dedicated to Adelyne, Grace, and Avery

A · TWODOT® · BOOK
An imprint of Globe Pequot
An imprint and registered trademark of Rowman & Littlefield

Distributed by NATIONAL BOOK NETWORK

British Library Cataloguing in Publication Information Available

Library of Congress Cataloging-in-Publication Data Available

ISBN 978-1-4930-0833-9 (paperback)
ISBN 978-1-4930-3066-8 (e-book)

∞™ The paper used in this publication meets the minimum requirements of American National Standard for Information Sciences—Permanence of Paper for Printed Library Materials, ANSI/ NISO Z39.48-1992.

CONTENTS

ACKNOWLEDGMENTS

THIS STUDY OF KATE WARNE AND THOSE WHO SERVED AS THE FIRST women operatives with the Pinkerton National Detective Agency benefited from the energy of many individuals. Librarian and historian Madelyn Helling inspired it, TwoDot editorial director Erin Turner encouraged it, and archivists at the Library of Congress and the Chicago Historical Society enriched it.

Special thanks to Rachel Dworkin, archivist at the Chemung County Historical Society, for supplying information about Kate Warne's early life.

I'm grateful to Jennifer Brathovde, librarian at the Library of Congress, and archivist Charlotte Richards at the National Archives for their help with compiling information about the cases the lady Pinkerton agents investigated. John Moriarty, vice president and general counsel at the Pinkerton National Detective Agency, assisted in tracking down documents relating to Allan Pinkerton and the formation of the Secret Service; and Doug Cunningham, director of operations at the Agency, kindly offered advice on where to acquire employment records and aliases used.

Accomplished author Corey Recko was generous with his time and writing talent. I referred to his exceptional book *A Spy for the Union: The Life and Execution of Timothy Webster* often.

I greatly appreciate the sharp eye and diligent, fact-checking services of editor B. Keith Williams. His efforts go a long way toward helping me to be confident about the historical accuracy of the product I submit to the publisher.

Finally, to the gifted people at TwoDot, from the project managers to the artists who design the book covers, thank you very much for your efforts.

FOREWORD

WHEN ALLAN PINKERTON FOUNDED THE PINKERTON DETECTIVE Agency in 1850, he not only became the world's first "private eye," he also established an organization that would set the global standard for investigative and security excellence for generations to come.

But the agency had only just begun the process of setting that standard when Kate Warne walked into Allan Pinkerton's office six years later and asked for a job. Her request was well timed. Pinkerton was keenly focused on new opportunities and was consciously looking to make bold choices that reinforced his vision of Pinkerton as an innovator and a disruptor.

Warne's confidence and persuasive skills were impressive, and Pinkerton's flexibility and willingness to "defy convention" perhaps equally so. It is to his credit, and to the enduring credit of the Pinkerton Detective Agency, that it took Pinkerton less than twenty-four hours to inform Warne that he would hire her—a decision that made her the nation's first female detective. It was a remarkable turn of events at a time when only 15 percent of women held jobs outside of the home, and contemporary ideas about what constituted "women's work" severely limited employment opportunities for women.

Kate Warne, and the accomplished women who played such an important role in building the Pinkerton Detective Agency into an iconic global security and law enforcement institution, made it abundantly clear that the prevailing definition of "women's work" was not just inadequate, but wholly obsolete.

Kate's story, and the stories of all of these remarkable female operatives—presented so beautifully and in such rich detail here in this fascinating and important book—are not just a moving reminder of the

Portrait of Allan Pinkerton, founder of the Pinkerton
National Detective Agency COURTESY OF THE LIBRARY OF
CONGRESS

achievements of a handful of bold pioneers, they are also a remarkable
testament to the exemplary tradition of innovation that has distinguished
the Pinkerton name over the course of more than a century and a half of
dedicated service.

Allan Pinkerton was very clear about the fact that he wanted his
company to be fearless and to have a "reputation for using innovative methods to achieve its goals." What is remarkable is not just the
aspiration, but the execution: This founding vision would grow into a
long-standing tradition of innovation and a commitment to inspired service that became intricately woven into Pinkerton's organizational DNA.

Pinkerton's enduring legacy of bold moves, brave choices, and the
relentless pursuit of excellence is much more than just an aging résumé—

it is the foundation for an organization that remains on the cutting edge. Today, the company that predates the Civil War not only remains relevant, but has continued to establish itself as a dynamic and innovative presence on the world stage. Pinkerton is a recognized industry leader in developing forward-looking security and risk management solutions for national and international corporations. Remarkably, an organization that once protected Midwestern railways and pursued famous outlaws like Jesse James and Butch Cassidy is now providing sophisticated corporate risk management strategies and high-level security services for clients across the globe, setting a twenty-first-century standard for corporate risk management.

Now, as then, Pinkerton understands that combating new and emerging threats and serving its clients require a willingness to challenge conventional wisdom, and embrace new assets and new ideas—whether they are the world's first female detectives or new cybersecurity protocols. From investigative and private detective work to security and corporate risk consulting, Pinkerton prides itself on doing whatever it takes to keep its clients safe and to protect their assets and their interests. That resolve is one of the biggest reasons why an agency that was protecting Abraham Lincoln was also on the ground in the aftermath of Hurricane Katrina, and why the principles and practices that were in place almost eighty years *before* the discovery of penicillin still apply to an organization that provides risk management services to some of the world's most innovative enterprises in 2016.

As you read and enjoy these fascinating profiles of gifted Pinkerton operatives, you will readily see how their work and their character exemplified the agency's values of Integrity, Vigilance, and Excellence. Ultimately, those attributes are at the heart of these tales, and at the heart of the larger Pinkerton story. It's a history that spans three centuries, with compelling new chapters still being written each and every day.

—Jack Zahran, president of the Pinkerton National Detective Agency

INTRODUCTION

HER SMILE COULD BE SHY, HER GLANCE AT TIMES DEMURE, BUT HER ears never missed a secret. She was a master of disguises who could change her accent at will, infiltrate social gatherings, and collect information no man was able to obtain. She cried on command, was stoic while interrogating a suspect, and composed when necessary. She was tough when needed, accommodating when warranted, and never, ever slept on the job. She was a detective working for the nation's first security service: the Pinkerton Detective Agency.

Allan Pinkerton, founder of the organization and pioneer in the field, dared to hire women as agents. Kate Warne, recognized by many historians as America's first female detective, persuaded Pinkerton to take a chance on her sleuthing skills in 1856. Prior to her being hired at the agency, women were relegated to secretarial duties at the company.

Allan Pinkerton was born on August 25, 1819, in Glasgow. His father, William Pinkerton, was a police sergeant in that city and died from injuries inflicted by a prisoner he was taking into custody. Until the age of thirty-three, Allan Pinkerton followed the trade of a cooper, which he learned in Scotland and subsequently practiced in Canada and the United States.

Pinkerton's search for a location and opening took him to Chicago and then to Dundee, Kane County, Illinois, thirty-eight miles from Chicago. He had a habit of making the wrongs of the community his own, and it led him to uncovering a ring of counterfeiters living and working in the area. All were captured and tried for their crimes.

The fame of this exploit, together with his success in capturing horse thieves on various occasions, gave Pinkerton a wide local reputation; he was made deputy sheriff of Kane County, in which capacity he soon became the terror of cattle thieves, horse thieves, counterfeiters, and mail robbers all over the state. He was a born detective with such rare genius for the craft and such an extraordinary personality that there was no keeping him in obscurity. Pinkerton parlayed his talent into his own company, established in 1850. He had an excellent instinct for selecting the right people to work for him. Kate Warne proved herself to be one of Pinkerton's finest agents and paved the way for other women detectives.

Over the course of Kate's twelve-year career as an agent, she used numerous aliases. She would spend months undercover assuming various roles, from a benevolent neighbor to an eccentric fortune-teller. Kate and other female investigators willingly put themselves in harm's way to resolve a case. Whether it was searching the home of a suspected murderer for clues or transporting classified material past armed soldiers, lady Pinkerton agents demonstrated that they were fearless and capable.

After a little more than four years, Kate had so impressed Pinkerton with her aptitude for investigation and observation that he made her the head of all female detectives at the agency. In early 1861, he placed her in charge of the Union Intelligence Service, a forerunner of the Secret Service. The function of the Secret Service was to obtain information about the Confederacy's resources and plans and to prevent such news from reaching the Rebel army. There, too, Kate and the other lady operatives excelled at their duties. According to Pinkerton's memoirs, potential recruits were made aware of how valuable Kate's work was to the organization. "In my service you will serve your country better than on the [battle]field," Pinkerton told hopeful employees. "I have several female operatives. If you agree to come aboard you will go in training with the head of my female detectives, Kate Warne. She has never let me down."

Among the key members of Kate's staff was Hattie Lawton, a dedicated supporter of the Union stationed in Washington, where she posed as the wife of the first spy in the Civil War to be executed. Accomplished sculptor Vinnie Ream was another operative. She acted as a spy inside the White House while creating a marble bust of President Lincoln. Mrs. E. H. Baker uncovered Confederate plans for the development of sophisticated weaponry that could have changed the course of the Civil War had it not been discovered. Masquerading as a nurse, Elizabeth Van

Lew supplied General Ulysses S. Grant with vital tactical and strategic information that gave the Yankees a decided edge over the Rebels.

It's difficult to fully research the career of a spy, as the very essence of their craft involves subterfuge and misdirection. If you're a good spy, few know anything at all about you. Agents spend several months at a time on covert missions. They might use the same alias for the entire job, or change their handle in the middle of a case if the investigation has been compromised. Pinkerton kept meticulous records of the work his operatives performed, but volumes of files stored at his Chicago office were destroyed in a fire in the early 1930s. What remained was eventually transferred to the National Archives and the Library of Congress. The trail of the operatives was charted using Pinkerton's records, newspaper articles, and memoirs of the various agents.

Critics of Pinkerton argue that he not only exaggerated his role in helping to solve the cases he undertook, but also invented the capers themselves to promote the agency and generate business. Pinkerton disregarded the insults and credited the comments to envious competitors.

Pinkerton was a sharp businessman who could not be bullied and who knew what battles were important to fight. In 1876, three of Pinkerton's top agents banded together to persuade him to reconsider hiring female detectives. Pinkerton learned that the request had been made at the urging of his male operatives' jealous wives. The men admitted their wives had difficulty with the idea of them working alongside women, but said their real reason for not wanting females at the company was the fact that the job had become too dangerous for women. Pinkerton was outraged and made his position clear. "It has been my principle to use females for the detection of crime where it has been useful and necessary," he announced. "With regard to the employment of such females, I can trace it back to the moment I first hired Kate Warne, up to the present time . . . and I intend to still use females whenever it can be done judiciously. I must do it or sacrifice my theory, practice, and truth. I think I am right, and if that is the case, female detectives must be allowed in my agency."

Pinkerton was loyal to the women he had hired. It was while working with Kate in 1861 that he came up with the idea for the company's logo

Pinkerton's National Detective Agency logo inspired by Operative Kate Warne COUR-TESY OF THE LIBRARY OF CONGRESS

and slogan: "We Never Sleep" is scrawled below an all-seeing eye. While on assignment to protect president-elect Abraham Lincoln, Kate refused to close her eyes and rest until the politician was out of danger.

More than one hundred years after the first female was hired by the Pinkerton Detective Agency, hundreds of women now work for the firm. Whether in plain clothes as investigators or in snappily tailored, steel-blue uniforms as security officers for industrial plants, colleges, hospitals, and convention centers, women fill a variety of assignments.

Like their predecessors, Lady Pinkertons (or Pinks for short) continue to be levelheaded and curious, as well as think-on-their-feet agents who know what to do in a crisis.

Although women were not admitted to any police force until 1891, or widely accepted as detectives until 1903, Kate Warne and the women she trained paved the way for future female officers and investigators, and are regarded as trailblazers in the private eye industry.

CHAPTER ONE

OPERATIVE
KATE WARNE

THE DEPOT OF THE PHILADELPHIA, WILMINGTON AND BALTIMORE
Railroad in Philadelphia was strangely bustling with an assortment of
customers on the evening of February 23, 1861.[1] Businessmen dressed in
tailcoats, high-waisted trousers, and elaborate cravats milled about with
laborers adorned in faded work pants, straw hats, and long dusters. Ladies
wearing long, flouncy, bell-shaped dresses and small hats topped with
ribbon streamers of blue, gold, and red mingled with women in plain
brown skirts, white leg o'mutton–sleeved blouses and shawls. Some of the
women traveled in pairs and conversed in low voices as they walked from
one side of the track to the other. Most everyone carried a carpetbag or
leather valise.

The depot was the hub of activity; parents and children, railroad
employees, and young men in military uniforms made their way with
tickets in hand and destinations in mind. Among the travelers were those
who were content to remain in one place, either on a bench reading a
paper or filling the wait time knitting. Some frequently checked their
watches, and others drummed their fingers on the wooden armrests of
their seats. There was an air of general anticipation. It was chilly and
damp, and restless ticket holders studied the sky for rain. In the far distance, thunder could be heard rumbling.[2]

At 10:50 in the evening, an engine and a few passenger cars pulled to
a stop at the depot, and a conductor disembarked. The man was pristinely

attired and neatly groomed. He removed a stopwatch from his pocket and cast a glance up and down the tracks before reading the time. The conductor made eye contact with a businessman standing near the ticket booth who nodded ever so slightly. The businessman adjusted the hat on his head and walked to the far end of the depot where a freight loader was pushing a cart full of luggage toward the train. The freight man eyed the businessman as he passed by, and the businessman turned and headed in the opposite direction. Something was about to happen, and the three individuals communicating in a minimal way were involved.

The woman's hand and wrist were hooked in the arm of a tall man, dark and lanky, wrapped in a heavy traveling shawl. He wore a broad-brimmed felt hat low on his head and was careful to look down as he hurried along. When he and his escort reached the car, the woman presented her tickets to the conductor, who had arrived on the scene at the same time. "My invalid brother and I are attending a family party," she volunteered. After examining the tickets for a moment, the conductor stepped aside to allow the pair to board. Protectively and tenderly, the woman took her brother's arm and helped him to the stairs leading up the train. With a hint of reluctance, the lean, angular man climbed aboard.[3]

The porter at the top of the steps kindly greeted the siblings and escorted them down a long, narrow passageway to their seats. The man and woman followed along obediently.

The conductor signaled the engineer and called out "All's well!" The three men in gray and black suits who had stepped off the train spanned out in different directions, one to the back of the passenger car, and two

2

of them heading toward the engine. The pair carefully surveyed the area around the vehicle, and when it seemed no one suspicious was loitering about, they jumped back on the train; as the train built up steam and pulled away from the station, the keen-eyed protectors continued to be on guard.[4]

Back inside, the porter deposited sister and brother in front of a double door that led to a sleeper car. The accommodations were modest, with an upper and lower berth on either side of the narrow walkway. The shades on the windows next to the berths were down so no one could see in or out. Allan Pinkerton, a hefty Scotsman with a beard and no mustache, considered the man and woman standing in the entrance of the car. After a brief, tense moment the tall man shed the shawl around his shoulders, removed his hat, and extended a hand to Allan to shake. Allan smiled slightly and took the man's hand. "Mr. Lincoln," he proudly responded. President-elect Abraham Lincoln responded with a grin. The politician turned to the woman next to him and handed her his shawl. "I am sensible, ma'am," he said sincerely, "of having put you to some inconvenience—not to speak of placing you in danger."[5]

"Kate . . . Mrs. Warne," Allan announced, "is one of the Pinkerton Agency's most competent detectives."

"I believe it has not hitherto been one of the prerequisites of the presidency to acquire in full bloom so charming and accomplished a female relation," Mr. Lincoln added.

Kate looked up into the kindly face of the president-elect and smiled graciously. The train whistle sounded, and Mr. Lincoln crowded himself and his worn, traveling bag into one of the berths. Kate took a seat on a bench between the president-elect and the door of the car. Her chief article of baggage was a loaded pistol.[6]

Chicago in the summer of 1856 was booming. Since its incorporation in 1837, it had grown from a moderately populated plains town to a major lake port and industrial center. Shipping and railroad lines were established there, and hotels, churches, and theaters mushroomed around the prosperous enterprises. The streets were continually crowded with people coming and going from the numerous houses being built. The sounds of sawing, hammering, and workmen shouting were common-

Chicago was experiencing explosive growth in the 1850s when Kate Warne entered the Pinkerton National Detective Agency with dreams of becoming an agent. COURTESY OF THE LIBRARY OF CONGRESS

place. With the growth in citizenry came a growth in crime. The need to restrain the increase in robberies and murders was great. Allan Pinkerton, a Scottish-born barrel maker turned law enforcement agent, established the first business to battle against such illegal activity.[7]

Allan Pinkerton and attorney Edward A. Rucker formed the Pinkerton Detective Agency in 1850, opening an office in the heart of Chicago. In letters to potential clients, they announced that the agency would attend to the "investigation and drepredation [*sic*] of frauds and criminal offenses; the detection of offenders, procuring arrests and convictions, apprehension, or return of fugitives from justice, or bail; recovering lost or stolen property, obtaining information, etc."[8]

In addition to Edward Rucker, Allan had a staff of a half-dozen capable men dedicated to ridding the city of outlaws that were terrorizing various communities. He was diligent about keeping records on the cases the company handled. Reviewing the material helped him to evaluate the strengths and weaknesses of the work the agency was doing, learn how to improve their success rate, and discover what new techniques needed to be employed to ensure an arrest.[9]

One early afternoon in 1856, Allan was reading over a file from one of the agency's most newsworthy cases. It was the capture of Jules Imbert, a famous French forger. Pinkerton agent George H. Bangs, a tall, fine-looking man of commanding presence and a close student of human nature, was the lead detective on the investigation. Imbert had obtained four drafts (a check drawn by a bank on its own funds in another bank) amounting to $15,000 from August Belmont and Company, a popular banking firm, and by forgeries had secured over $30,000 from unsuspecting New York bankers, after which he had fled the country. He was traced by George to Canada and captured.[10]

With no effort at subterfuge, George accused Imbert directly of forging checks, and by sheer pluck managed to get the criminal to confess to his crime. Once Imbert had confessed, the Pinkerton agent and his prisoner started for home via the train. George fastened the forger's right wrist to his own with his handcuffs. After traveling a hundred miles, Imbert drifted off to sleep. George, who was exhausted, followed suit. When he awoke he found, to his irritation, that the Frenchman had picked the lock of the handcuffs and escaped.[11]

The last stop the train made before entering the United States was a station called Fonda. George felt sure the prisoner had left the car at this point. George had the train stopped and retraced the distance on foot. It was late at night, and he went to the main hotel in town and asked for a bed, intending to begin his search in the morning. The hotel clerk said George's only option was to share a bed already occupied by a recent arrival. Glad to sleep anywhere, George accepted the offer.

When he turned down the coverlet of the bed, he saw, to his astonishment and delight, that his companion was his recent prisoner. He quickly subdued Imbert, and the following morning the pair boarded a train and returned safely to New York. Imbert was tried, convicted, and sent to state prison, where he died eight years later.

George had been lucky in the recapture of the forger, but Allan didn't like to depend on good fortune in apprehending suspects. He was pondering how much the company had progressed since starting the agency when his secretary announced that a young woman was waiting to see him. Allan rose to his feet as the slender, brown-eyed woman entered his office. Kate Warne politely introduced herself. She was bold and unintimidated. Allan described her in his memoirs as a lady "graceful in movement and self-possessed." He also wrote, "Her features, although not what could be called handsome, were decidedly of an intellectual cast. Her face was honest, which would cause one in distress instinctively to select her as a confidante."[12]

Kate had come to the Pinkerton Detective Agency in search of a job. She was a widow with no children, and had definite ideas about what she wanted to do for work. Allan assumed she was searching for a job as a secretary. He was surprised to learn that Kate was not looking for clerical work, but actually answering an advertisement for detectives he had placed in one of the Chicago newspapers. "It was not the custom to employ women detectives," Allan later wrote. "Indeed, I'd never heard of a female detective." He did not immediately dismiss the notion, and Kate wouldn't have let him if he'd tried; she was that determined. She explained quite persuasively how she could be of service. "Women could be most useful in worming out secrets in many places which would be impossible for a male detective," Allan remembered her saying. "A woman would be able to befriend the wives and girlfriends of suspected criminals and gain their confidence. Men become braggarts when they are around women who encourage them to boast. Women have an eye for detail and are excellent observers."

Kate had clearly thought this through, and Allan could see the rationale behind granting her request, but he asked her for twenty-four hours to consider having a woman on his payroll.

Allan was a keen businessman. His vision for the agency was for the public to see that being a detective was a profession and not merely an occupation. Allan was creating a unique service that would command a great respect for the trade. Men in his employ were referred to as operatives, and not detectives. Detectives, particularly in the Chicago area, were seen as abusive police officers who looked for evidence to solve a crime. Corrupt law enforcement officers weren't opposed to bending the rules to get their man. Operatives were to behave in a more dignified manner, to be beyond reproach, and possess refined skills. An operative could be an expert in handwriting analysis, disguises, or tracking. The Pinkertons would come to specialize in not only getting their man or woman, but also noticing the criminals' giveaway characteristics or distinguishing marks, with a novelist's eye for description.[13]

Allan expected his operatives to be well-groomed and polite. He maintained detailed records of the subject or situation his staff was charged with investigating and the clients who hired them, and he expected the same meticulous note-taking from those working for the Pinkerton Detective Agency. Allan believed procedures and priorities combined would define the industry and elevate the trade to one of great respectability. He wasn't opposed to defying convention to improve the agency. He wanted the company to have a reputation for using innovative methods to achieve its goals. That was one of the motivating factors that led to his agreeing to hire a woman.

When Kate Warne arrived back at Allan's office the following day and learned he would give her a job, she became the nation's first female detective. As was the standard, Allan started a file on the ambitious lady operative that included a variety of pertinent information about her life before becoming an agent.

According to the March 21, 1868, edition of the *Philadelphia Press*, Kate Warne was born in 1830 in the town of Erin Chemung County, New York. Her parents, Israel and Elizabeth Hulbert, struggled financially, and Kate had few opportunities for education. She married at a young age and was widowed by early 1856. She then moved to Illinois with her parents and her brother Allan. Kate realized the importance of finding employment if she were to support herself and provide some income for her family. Her first job in the city was as a house cleaner, but it was unsatisfying to her. Kate wanted to prove herself at a position that challenged her mind.[14] The *McArthur Enquirer* from March 19, 1868, referred to her as a "marked woman among her sex, with a large, active brain, great mental power, an excellent judge of character, strong active vitality." The Pinkerton Detective Agency was precisely the employment her "active brain" required.[15]

The detective agency Kate so fearlessly approached for a job was contracted by several prominent railroad lines to guard the rolling stock transported across the Midwestern frontier. The company provided police protection for the Illinois Central, Michigan Central, Michigan Southern and Northern Indiana, Galena and Chicago Union, Chicago and Rock Island, and Chicago, Burlington and Quincy Railroads.[16] The Pinkerton Detective Agency received retainers of various amounts to secure the passengers and property aboard the train. Pinkerton agreed in writing to have on hand a "sufficient number of reliable, active, and experienced assistants, to enable the agency to respond to the call of any; or either of the said companies without delay, and in case the business of either of them shall be of an unusually urgent character, and needing either more assistants or those having different qualifications than those then in their employ, they shall procure as soon as practical as many as may be needed." Allan classified the hiring of Kate as "procuring the assistants of those having different qualities."[17]

Kate Warne joined a staff of nine operatives, including Allan Pinkerton. Men employed by the agency were Timothy Webster, a former New York City police officer; Pryce Lewis, a former book salesman; John Scully, a quick-witted British gentleman who was prone to drinking too much; John H. White, regarded by Allan as a shrewd hand; John Fox, a former watchmaker from New England; Adam Roche, a German known as the Flying Dutchman, whose only vice was tobacco; R. Rivers, a tenacious, athletic man who would jog twelve miles rather than lose sight of a suspect's carriage; and a thirty-five-year-old gentleman named De Forest. He was tall, remarkably good-looking, with long black hair. He was known as a perfect "lady killer." George Bangs, Allan Pinkerton's keen and resourceful right-hand man, was also a member of the staff.[18]

In addition to the normal duties and responsibilities the Pinkerton Detective Agency had with the railroad lines, the company also worked with attorneys, law enforcement departments, and government representatives. Cases were subject to careful scrutiny before Allan would accept them. His operatives received a copy of a document he referred to as "general principles." It outlined the prerequisites for accepting a case. The agency would not represent a defendant in a criminal case except with the knowledge and consent of the prosecutor; they would not shadow jurors or investigate public officials in the performance of their duties or trade-union officers or members in their lawful union activities; they would not accept employment from one political party against another; they wouldn't report union meetings unless the meetings were open to the public without restrictions; they would not work for vice crusaders; they would not accept contingency fees, gratuities, or rewards. The agency would never investigate the morals of a woman unless in connection with another crime, nor would it handle cases of divorce or of a scandalous nature.[19]

Allan Pinkerton and his brother Robert helped to establish offices not only in Chicago, but in New York, Baltimore, and Wisconsin, as well. The September 6, 1856, edition of the *Janesville Daily Gazette* explained that securing offices in various locations not only enlarged the Pinkerton Detective Agency's field of operation, but also provided the company with an extensive familiarity with the geography of the country. "It also gave them an intimate connection with the police of other areas, which enabled them to operate with unparalleled success in any part of the country," the *Gazette* boasted.[20] The article continued:

A concern like theirs is of incalculable benefit to the commercial community and to the authorities of the numerous small towns, whose means do not enable them to maintain a regular police force. A timely application to Pinkerton and Company would enable them to get rid of the thieves and swindlers of various degrees who often make the smaller towns the field of their operations.[21]

Pinkerton and Company work quietly but efficiently, their detectives are shrewd, well drilled, and intelligent, and capable of adapting themselves to the circumstances of those upon whom they wish to operate.[22]

A certain place is infested with thieves, or has been the scene of depredation. A stranger appears in the neighborhood. He may appear to be a businessman, a speculator sporting man, a rowdy, a loafer, a thief—it matters not which. In a short time after his appearance, the officers who could previously obtain no clue to the depredators, now easily find them out, and when they are secured or cleared out, the stranger disappears also. He was a detective.[23]

Kate Warne was assigned to a case within two days of being made an operative. Some historians argue that Kate's early ambition to become an actress played a part in her success as a detective. She was able to play a variety of roles while investigating criminal suspects. Perhaps she expressed her love of acting to Pinkerton during her initial interview and assured him she was capable of hiding her true identity while working a case. In-depth records about that meeting were destroyed in a fire in 1871. What is known is that Pinkerton saw something in Kate he believed would make a fine investigator. Decades after his first encounter with Kate, Pinkerton wrote in his memoirs that "she succeeded far beyond my utmost expectations."[24]

Kate's involvement in the investigation of an employee of the Adams Express Company, a freight and cargo transportation line that ran throughout the Southeast, was documented by Pinkerton in a case he called "The Expressman and the Detective."[25]

The Adams Express Company was founded in 1854 and began personal delivery of securities, documents, and parcels between the financial centers of Boston and New York. The company expanded rapidly, first throughout the South and Southeast, and, in time, westward.[26]

In 1855 Allan Pinkerton received a letter from Edward S. Sanford, vice president of the Adams Express Company, explaining that $10,000 had been stolen from a locked money pouch somewhere between their Montgomery, Alabama, headquarters and a branch office in Augusta, Georgia. Sanford wanted the agency to find the thief. Pinkerton's initial assessment of the robbery was that someone from the inside had absconded with the money. He shared his thought with Sanford in a letter of reply, and had not heard again from the businessman for more than a year. In the summer of 1856, Pinkerton received an urgent message from Sanford requesting that the famous detective please hurry to meet him in Alabama. Pinkerton did as he asked.[27]

A frantic Sanford met Pinkerton and George Bangs at the train depot in Montgomery and told them another $40,000 had been stolen. Sanford informed the pair that he'd had someone closely watching the activities at the Adams Express Company office there, and didn't believe it was an "inside job." Nathan Maroney, manager of the Montgomery office, had placed the money in a sealed pouch before sending it to the New York office. By the time the pouch had reached its destination, the money was gone. The October 6, 1883, edition of the *Oshkosh Daily Northwestern* reported that "a square hole, a clean cut made by a razor, was in the side of the bag, concealed from the public view by the outer pocket of the pouch."

At first, Sanford and his immediate staff considered the possibility that the funds had been taken by a messenger. Each of a dozen messengers employed at the company were investigated, but all of them seemed to be trustworthy and didn't appear to have done anything wrong. Although Nathan Maroney had an impeccable reputation and was well liked in the community, both Pinkerton and George Bangs believed he was the most likely suspect.

Nathan was from Texas originally, and had fought in the Mexican War alongside a company of Texas Rangers. Since moving to Montgomery in 1851, he had worked for a competing stage line known as Hampton and Company. He had also worked as a treasurer for a circus. The circus disbanded after going bankrupt. It was alleged but never proven that Nathan had embezzled money from the circus. A job as a conductor on a railroad had led to a position at Adams Express Company, the management of which decided to watch Nathan for a time to see if he might lead them to the money they suspected he'd stolen.[28]

In the fall of 1858, Nathan took a leave of absence from Adams Express Company and traveled to cities in the East and the Northwest. Unaware that he was being followed, detectives observed that he spent a great deal of money on "high living." He purchased expensive clothes for himself and his wife, stayed in the finest hotels, and invested in racehorses. His actions prompted an arrest. Nathan was charged with stealing $40,000.[29]

The population of Montgomery was outraged. The ex–Adams Express Company employee was so revered that the townspeople criticized the company's management for having him taken into custody. Pinkerton later wrote of the incident that the public claimed it was "another instance of the persecution of a poor man by a powerful corporation to cover the carelessness of those high in authority and thus turn the blame on some innocent person." Prominent townspeople believed so firmly in Nathan's innocence that they signed his bail bond.[30]

The case against Nathan was indeed weak. Without the assistance of the Pinkerton Detective Agency, not only would the suspect go free, but none of the stolen money would be recovered. Physical evidence linking Nathan to the crime was imperative.[31]

Pinkerton initially assigned six of his most capable operatives to get to the bottom of the case. Among those operatives were George Bangs, John White, Adam Roche, John Fox, and Kate Warne. White's job was to establish himself in the community and learn all he could about Nathan Maroney. Roche was supposed to shadow Nathan's wife. John Fox was to set up a watch shop near Nathan's parents' home in Pennsylvania, in case the accused visited and possibly tried to hide the money on the property. Kate Warne, who took on the identity of the wife of a wealthy forger, was to befriend Nathan's wife. A background investigation on Mrs. Maroney revealed she was from a respectable family, and that prior to marrying Nathan, she was a widow with one child. As a young woman, she had run away from home and fallen in with fast crowds in New Orleans, Charleston, South Carolina, and Augusta, Georgia. She had met Nathan in Mobile, Alabama, and the two had been married shortly thereafter.[32]

Working in concert, the operatives assigned to the case uncovered Nathan's fondness for gambling, primarily on horses. Pinkerton believed that the compulsive habit had left the suspect in dire straits financially, and that he'd stolen the money from Adams Express Company to cover his debts, or future gambling sprees. "It is impossible for the human mind to retain a secret," Pinkerton wrote of the investigation years later. The plan was to supply Nathan and his wife with confidants in whom they would entrust their secrets.[33]

At Pinkerton's suggestion, a decision was made by the attorneys for the Adams Express Company to have Nathan rearrested on a charge of conspiracy. A so-called forger was arrested along with Nathan; of course, he wasn't really a forger at all, but operative John White. Pretending to be a courier, White was placed in a cell with Nathan. George Bangs posed as John White's attorney.[34]

Nathan's wife was not in town when he was placed into custody a second time, and subsequently moved to New York; she was in Pennsylvania, visiting family. While she was there, she made the acquaintance of a handsome young man named Mr. De Forest, who seemed quite taken with her. He was complimentary of her looks and manner of dress. Mrs. Maroney was flattered and accepted invitations to dine with the stranger. She was unaware that he, too, was a Pinkerton operative. Prior to Mrs. Maroney's return to Montgomery, anonymous letters were sent to Nathan about his wife and the company she was keeping. He shared his dismay over the situation with John White. John listened sympathetically to his cellmate's concerns about his marriage. When Mrs. Maroney came to visit her husband in jail, he asked her about the rumor. She admitted to keeping company with the flattering suitor, but assured her husband they were nothing more than friends.[35]

Consumed with worry and frustrated that he was in jail and unable to intercede, Nathan prevailed upon George Bangs to help him. He believed that Bangs was an attorney, and had overheard him bragging to John White that the mind of the courts could always be changed provided an offender had enough money to do so. George promised to represent Nathan, but told him the price for taking care of the situation would be high. Nathan sent for his wife and instructed her to retrieve the stolen money to pay for the lawyer.[36]

Mrs. Maroney left the jail perplexed. She wasn't sure if she should surrender the money or keep it for herself. She needed to discuss the matter with someone. Mrs. Maroney recalled a woman she had spent time with in Pennsylvania during her stay. She had met her at the Merchants' Hotel, and the two had become fast friends. The woman was kind,

Many have mistakenly identified the person leaning against the tent stake in the center as Kate Warne. The men in the photo are: (seated) R. William Moore and Allan Pinkerton; (standing) George H. Bangs, John C. Babcock, and Augustus K. Uttlefield. COURTESY OF THE LIBRARY OF CONGRESS

thoughtful, and generous. It was as if the women had known each other for several years and were free to talk about anything without fear of reproach. The woman Mrs. Maroney felt she could consult called herself Madam Imbert. She portrayed herself as a polished, well-spoken lady of high-class society. In actuality, she was Kate Warne.[37]

Pinkerton recalled in his case files the chain of events leading to the two women's not-so-chance encounter. "Madam Imbert, along with another woman named Miss Johnson, drove out to Jenkintown [Pennsylvania] and passed a couple of days at the tavern," Pinkerton noted. "They found that the rooms at the adjoining hotel, though plain, were very neatly kept and that the table was abundantly supplied with good, substantial food. Madam Imbert expressed herself well satisfied with the town, the purity of the air, and its beautiful drives and walks; and as her system had become rather debilitated by a long residence in the South, she thought she would spend the summer there, recuperating from her failing health. She made an arrangement with the landlord to spend the summer at his house, drove into Philadelphia, and reported to me. She had her baggage sent out, and the following day returned with Miss Johnson and they took up their abode in the tavern. It was here they made the acquaintance of Mrs. Maroney."[38]

Mr. De Forest was visiting with Mrs. Maroney when Madam Imbert saw the woman for the first time. Madam Imbert was pleased to see how well Mr. De Forest had charmed his way into Mrs. Maroney's good graces, and realized that Mrs. Maroney was struggling to keep her feelings for the handsome operative in check. Madam Imbert stealthily followed Mr. De Forest, Mrs. Maroney, and her daughter, Flora, as they strolled around the grounds of the hotel. Flora ran ahead of the couple, and when she turned to run back to her mother, the little girl tripped on a path near where Madam Imbert was standing. Madam Imbert helped the child to her feet and brushed the dirt and gravel from her knees and hands. Mrs. Maroney hurried to Flora and scooped her up into her arms. She introduced herself to Madam Imbert and expressed her sincere thanks for being kind to her daughter.[39]

The following day Mrs. Maroney and Madam Imbert had lunch together, then took a brisk walk and talked. Madam Imbert confided in her new friend that she had been traveling through the South in hopes that a change from her usual routine would bring her out of the melancholy mood from which she was suffering. Mrs. Maroney felt sorry for Madam Imbert and determined to find out the reason for her being so sad. Mrs. Maroney noticed that Madam Imbert received many letters, and that each time they were delivered to the hotel, the woman broke into tears. The two quickly became good friends, and Madam Imbert eventually shared the reason for her unhappiness: She missed her husband.[40]

"Mrs. Maroney," Madam Imbert sobbed, "I fear you find me poor company, indeed." Pinkerton reported in the tale of "the Expressman and the Detective" that Kate played the part of a lady in distress perfectly. "You have a kind husband, a sweet child, everything that makes life enjoyable. While I am separated from my dear husband, far away, with no one to love me! No one to care for me! I have bitter trouble, rendered all the harder to bear by the fact that I have to brood over it alone. I have not one friend in this wide world to whom I can fly for consolation. No! Not one! My life is unspeakably lonely. You will forgive me for not being more gay. I cannot help it! I strive to be, but it is impossible. I often fear that my melancholy has a chilling effect on those around me, and that you think me cold and heartless!"[41]

"Madam Imbert—my dear madam," Mrs. Maroney is noted to have said, "don't you say that you are thought to be cold and heartless! Everyone feels that you are suffering some great sorrow, and all are drawn toward you. As for me, I have always tried to secure the sympathy of my lady friends, but I have only half succeeded. You are the first one in whom I have ever felt that I could confide, the first whom I wished to be my friend. If you are in trouble and feel the need of a friend, why not rely on me? Make me your confidante."

Kate would later tell Pinkerton that she was pleased Mrs. Maroney was moved by her act.

"My story is a sad one," Madam Imbert sobbed. "I already value our friendship too highly to risk losing it. If you were to know my history, I fear you would turn from me in disgust."[42]

Madam Imbert's tears flowed freely, and she leaned on Mrs. Maroney for support. Mrs. Maroney turned into one of the side paths and they took a seat on a bench. After much persuasion, Kate knew it was time for Madam Imbert to disclose her secret. She told Mrs. Maroney that her husband was a forger convicted for his crimes and sentenced to ten years in prison. She wept aloud while explaining that she had been barred from seeing him by the courts. Mrs. Maroney was understanding and tried her best to comfort her distressed friend.[43]

Madam Imbert thanked Mrs. Maroney for her kindness, and Mrs. Maroney shared that she, too, had a husband who was persecuted and "in the throws [sic] of severe trouble." Unaware of what had transpired, Mr. De Forest arrived on the tender scene to escort Mrs. Maroney on their daily constitutional. He asked the women if they were all right and inquired about what was the matter, but neither offered an explanation.

Before the party separated, Madam Imbert assured Mrs. Maroney they would see one another soon. She was right; less than twenty-four hours after their last meeting, Mrs. Maroney visited Madam Imbert at her hotel room. Mrs. Maroney informed her that she was going south for a visit but would return shortly. She did not mention anything about going back to Montgomery, but Madam Imbert felt certain that was where she was headed.[44]

Pinkerton operatives in Montgomery spotted Mrs. Maroney when she came to town and followed her and her daughter to the Exchange Hotel, where they registered to stay. She called on friends of her husband's, but none were as cordial to her as they had been before. The townspeople who once believed Nathan was a fine, upstanding citizen had changed their minds about him and his wife. Pinkerton agents never let Mrs. Maroney out of their sight. They hoped she would lead them to the stolen money. Instead, Mrs. Maroney made her way back to Pennsylvania and to Madam Imbert at the Merchants' Hotel.[45]

According to Pinkerton's detailed account of the case, Mrs. Maroney finally broke down and confessed to Madam Imbert that her husband was a prisoner being held in New York at the instigation of the Adams Express Company, who had charged him with having robbed them of some $50,000. Mrs. Maroney told Madam Imbert that the only friend she had was the abundance of money her husband had left her. Madam Imbert tried to coax the conversation along. She believed the longer Mrs. Maroney talked, the more likely she would be to reveal the location of the abundance of funds she had mentioned. Mrs. Maroney could not be persuaded to keep talking; she wanted to write a letter to her husband, explaining where she was and what had transpired.[46]

When Mrs. Maroney left to write her letter, Madam Imbert snuck out of the hotel to tell the other Pinkerton operatives in town to intercept Mrs. Maroney's correspondence. The letter was quite telling. In it, Mrs. Maroney assured her husband that she had retrieved the money from the hiding place and stored it in a safe place, somewhere else.[47]

The two women continued to meet and talk. Mrs. Maroney grew to trust Madam Imbert more and more. Mrs. Maroney eventually asked Madam Imbert to travel to New York with her to meet her husband in prison. Madam Imbert was more than happy to oblige. Nathan Maroney was as impressed with Madam Imbert as his wife; after their visit with him, Nathan told Mrs. Maroney that Madam Imbert was a trustworthy individual, and that she should feel free to solicit help from her.[48]

Not long after their visit with Nathan, Mrs. Maroney confessed all to Madam Imbert (Kate), who later reported Mrs. Maroney's words to Pinkerton: "My husband took the $40,000 from the Express Company, and also $10,000 previously. Now all is out!" Mrs. Maroney continued: "When he was thrown into prison in New York, he sent me for the money, which he had concealed in Montgomery, and I brought it here and have hidden it in a cellar. Nathan wants me to turn it over to a friend and his attorney. But if I do that I'll never see it again. In fact, I'm sure I never shall."[49]

"You're mistaken," Madam Imbert assured her. "Have confidence."

"Confidence?" she is noted to have said. "It would be best to run away myself!"[50]

Madam Imbert managed to talk Mrs. Maroney out of the idea of running away, and implored her to surrender the funds to the people her husband had indicated. Finally, Mrs. Maroney escorted Madam Imbert to a home with a cellar where the money was buried.[51]

Madam Imbert helped her to dig the treasure out of the ground. It was eighteen inches under the level of the cellar floor, wrapped in a piece of oilskin. The money was then turned over to the Pinkerton operative acting as a courier for Nathan's lawyer, George Bangs. The stolen money was transferred back to the Adams Express Company. With the exception of $485.00, which had already been spent by Nathan Maroney, all the funds were recovered.[52]

Nathan Maroney was returned to Montgomery to stand trial for the theft of the Adams Express Company funds. Just prior to the money being retrieved, Nathan confessed the robbery to his cellmate. The cellmate, who was also a Pinkerton operative, testified against the former express agent. In June 1860, Nathan was sentenced to ten years' imprisonment in the Alabama penitentiary. No charges were filed against Mrs. Maroney, who decided to move to Chicago with her daughter.[53]

Madam Imbert returned to Chicago as well. She and Mrs. Maroney drifted apart, and eventually Madam Imbert faded away. Kate Warne had proven herself to be a valuable asset to the Pinkerton Detective Agency, and would continue her good work for years to come.

Notes

1. Stashower, *The Hour of Peril*, pp. 252–56; Horan, *The Pinkertons: The Detective Dynasty that Made History*, pp. 52–57; Moran, *The Eye That Never Sleeps*, 38–42; *Fayetteville Semi-Weekly Observer*, February 28, 1861.

2. "Introducing Charles Rawn, His Journals, and Their Editors," The Rawn Journals 1830–1865 (dauphincountyhistory.org/backups/rawn/about/).

3. *San Antonio Light*, February 11, 1951.

4. Stashower, *The Hour of Peril*, pp. 252–56; Horan, *The Pinkertons*, pp. 52–57; Moran, *The Eye That Never Sleeps*, pp. 38–42; *Fayetteville Semi-Weekly Observer*, February 28, 1861.

5. *Fayetteville Semi-Weekly Observer*, February 28, 1861.

6. Ibid.

7. Horan, *The Pinkertons*, pp. 25–27.

8. *Journal News*, December 14, 1975.

9. Horan, *The Pinkertons*, pp. 25–27; *The Times*, November 8, 1883.

10. *Columbus Herald*, November 23, 1883; Horan, *The Pinkertons*, pp. 26–27.

11. Horan, *The Pinkertons*, pp. 26–27; *The Morning News*, November 24, 1883.

12. Horan, *The Pinkertons*, pp. 52–61; Moran, *The Eye That Never Sleeps*, pp. 54–55.

13. *Elyria Chronicle Telegram*, January 3, 1982.

14. *Philadelphia Press*, March 21, 1868.

15. *McArthur Enquirer*, March 19, 1868.

16. Horan, *The Pinkertons*, pp. 31–36.

17. Ibid.

18. Ibid.

19. Ibid.

20. *Janesville Daily Gazette*, September 6, 1856.

21. Ibid.

22. Ibid.

23. Ibid.

24. Horan, *The Pinkertons*, pp. 29–33.

25. Pinkerton, *The Expressman and the Detective*, pp. 3–7; "The Express Companies," Midcontinent.org (www.midcontinent.org/rollingstock/dictionary/express_companies.htm).

26. "The Express Companies."

27. Pinkerton, *The Expressman and the Detective*, pp. 7–8.

28. Ibid.

29. Ibid.

30. Ibid., pp. 8–11.
31. Ibid.
32. Ibid., pp. 10–15.
33. Ibid.
34. Ibid., pp. 17–26.
35. Ibid.
36. Ibid.
37. Ibid., pp. 21–25.
38. Ibid.
39. Ibid., pp. 38–53.
40. Ibid.
41. Ibid.
42. Ibid., pp. 57–62.
43. Ibid.
44. Ibid.
45. Ibid.
46. *Public Ledger*, July 4, 1860; *Oshkosh Daily Northwestern*, October 6, 1883.
47. Pinkerton, *The Expressman and the Detective*, pp. 62–67.
48. Ibid.
49. Ibid.
50. Ibid., pp. 69–74.
51. Ibid.
52. Ibid., pp. 82–101.
53. Pinkerton, *The Expressman and the Detective*, pp. 82–101; *Alabama Daily Confederation*, June 22, 1860; *Public Ledger*, June 4, 1860.

CHAPTER TWO

OPERATIVE
MRS. R. C. POTTER

IN THE SPRING OF 1858, A FRIENDLY, TWO-HORSE RACE ATTRACTED THE attention of many residents in the town of Atkinson, Mississippi. Mrs. Franklin Robbins and Mrs. R. C. Potter, both guests at one of the community's finest hotels, had decided to see which one of their mounts was the fastest. They had begun their afternoon ride in the company of several others, enjoying the balmy air, blooming flowers, and waving foliage of the sunny, Southern landscape. Exploring a path that led to a bubbling stream, Mrs. Robbins and Mrs. Potter had lagged far behind the party. They decided to narrow the gap when talk about who could make that happen first arose.[1]

For a few moments, both the horses the women were riding ran at an uneven but steady pace; then suddenly Mrs. Robbins's horse bolted ahead. Her ride didn't stop until they had reached the business district of town. Mrs. Robbins slowed the flyer to a trot before she glanced back to check on her competitor. Mrs. Potter was nowhere to be seen. Mrs. Robbins backtracked a bit, her eyes scanning the road she'd traveled. Her horse reared and threatened to continue the run, but she restrained the animal and pulled tightly on the reins. "Mrs. Potter!" she called out frantically. "Mrs. Potter?"

Mrs. Robbins's urgent cries drew the attention of the people with whom the pair had started the ride. They had congregated in front of the hotel when they heard Mrs. Robbins call for help. Not only did the fellow riders hurry to the scene, but men and women at various stores and saloons also rushed to Mrs. Robbins's aid.

Through her tears she explained what had transpired and asked volunteers to accompany her in search of Mrs. Potter. Many quickly agreed, and wasted no time in following Mrs. Robbins. She spurred her horse back along the roadway they had just traveled. The riders spread out in hopes of finding a trail leading to where Mrs. Potter's mount might have carried her.

One rider spotted a woman's scarf caught in the low-hanging branch of an oak tree and made his find public. Tracks near the tree led searchers to believe Mrs. Potter's horse might have been spooked and out of control. After several tense moments trekking back and forth over field and stream, Mrs. Potter was located. She had been thrown from her ride and was lying motionless in a meadow adjacent to the home of the county clerk, Alexander Drysdale.

Mrs. Robbins rode to Drysdale's house and informed him of what had happened. In less than five minutes, he had improvised a stretcher out of a wicker settee and a mattress and had summoned four of his hired hands to help retrieve the injured Mrs. Potter. She was groaning in pain. She told those attending to her that her head hurt. In a few moments, the hired hands had lifted her off the ground and gently placed her in the settee. While being carried to Drysdale's home, Mrs. Potter complained that her ribs were sore and her back was aching. Mr. Drysdale sent Mrs. Robbins and the other riders on their way and requested that Mrs. Robbins return with a physician. He promised that he and his wife would keep Mrs. Potter comfortable while waiting for the doctor to arrive.

Mrs. Potter was grateful for the Drysdales' consideration and thanked them over and over again. The hired hands were instructed to put the injured woman in one of the guest bedrooms and see to her every need.

When the physician arrived, he examined Mrs. Potter but could not determine the extent of her injuries. He recommended that she remain in bed and not be moved. He didn't think she would need to be confined to bed rest for more than two weeks. Mrs. Potter asked if she could be moved to the hotel, as she did not want to take advantage of the Drysdales' hospitality. Mrs. Drysdale, however, refused to hear of such a thing as the removal of a sick person from her house, and said that she would enjoy Mrs. Potter's company. Mrs. Potter agreed to stay with the Drysdales until she could move about without assistance.

No one suspected that Mrs. Potter was an operative for the Pinkerton Detective Agency. They had no idea her real name was Kate Warne, and that she had been tasked with infiltrating the Drysdales' home to locate a murderer. As Mrs. Potter, Kate had pretended that her horse had been frightened and out of control, eventually throwing her—that she'd been deposited purely by chance near the Drysdales' house, and that the injuries sustained in the fall were substantial enough to render her too fragile to move.

Mrs. Potter had arrived in Atkinson, Mississippi, with another operative acting as her father and using the name Mr. C. B. Rockwell, less than two weeks prior to the riding mishap. The fine-looking, white-haired gentleman had remained in town long enough to see that the woman portraying his daughter was nicely settled at the hotel. Once he was satisfied that she was comfortable and didn't need him, he left. Mr. Rockwell told the proprietors of the hotel that he had to return to their home in Jacksonville, Florida, as his business required his immediate assistance.

Mrs. Potter, described by guests as a "distinguished-looking brunette," claimed to be a widow with no children. According to Pinkerton, "she was tall and graceful, and her entertaining conversation made her a general favorite among the ladies at the hotel." She was not an invalid, but she told people the family physician had recommended she escape the rainy, foggy weather of Florida and take in the dry air of northern Mississippi for a few months. Mrs. Potter made friends easily and was much sought after by her fellow guests. Her true motive for her congenial disposition was to acquire information about the townspeople who came and went, and to ascertain which individuals behaved suspiciously, and why.

Allan Pinkerton began his notes on this case that involved Kate Warne with news of a letter he had received from Thomas McGregor, cashier of the City Bank of Atkinson. Thomas had been asked by bank officials to write Pinkerton for help in solving a brutal killing.

A teller by the name of George Gordon had been slain, and $130,000 stolen. Pinkerton hurried from Chicago to Mississippi to investigate. He traveled to Atkinson using an assumed name and claimed to be a cotton speculator; only Thomas McGregor and two other key representatives of the bank knew his true identity. In order to familiarize himself with the town and some of the people who lived there, Pinkerton roamed about Atkinson for a few hours before stopping by the bank. McGregor met Pinkerton when he arrived at the business and then introduced him to the bank president, Peter Gordon, no relation to George Gordon, and the vice president, a Mr. Bannatine.

All three men described the victim, George Gordon, as an industrious man with an obliging disposition and courteous manners. He had a spotless character and forfeited any leisure time in favor of work. George had been with the bank for five years. Pinkerton asked if he had any questionable friends or if he'd been involved romantically with any "fast" women, and was told that George kept mainly to himself and was "unencumbered by female companionship." He had a habit of remaining in the bank after office hours to maintain the books. Not only was he a teller, but he also acted as bookkeeper. His working late to accommodate regular customers who came in with a deposit wasn't unusual.

Two customers in particular had a habit of coming late to the bank when George was on duty. One was a jeweler named Mr. Flanders. McGregor informed Pinkerton that Mr. Flanders liked to put his most valuable pieces of jewelry in the bank at the close of his workday. The second customer was the county clerk, Alexander Drysdale, who used to stop by to make deposits when parties had paid money to him after banking hours. Alexander and George were friends, sometimes sitting and visiting together until nine or ten in the evening.

As Pinkerton's questions continued, he learned that George always had a set of vault keys with him. McGregor told Pinkerton that he had warned George against carrying the keys home with him. During harvest season, a large amount of money was kept at the bank, and bank executives worried that someone might try to take the keys from him. George assured the men he would be careful. A week after their discussion, George was found murdered.

Mr. Peter Gordon described the scene of the crime to Pinkerton in great detail. George's body was found in the morning when Mr. Gordon arrived at work at ten in the morning. He knew immediately something was wrong because the doors were still locked. Mr. Gordon's clerk arrived on the scene just as he was entering through an unlocked side door. As the two men were preparing to open for business, they found George's body on the floor between his desk and the vault door. The direction of the blood spray indicated that he had been standing at his desk when he was struck from behind.

George had received three blows to the back of his head with a hammer. The hammer was lying near his body, covered with blood and hair. According to Pinkerton's notes, the first blow was dealt just in back of the left ear while George was standing at his desk; he had staggered backwards two or three steps before falling, and the second and third blows had been struck as he lay on the floor.

"The scene was most ghastly," Mr. Gordon conveyed to Pinkerton. "George's body lay in a pool of blood, while the desks, chairs, table, and wall were splattered with large drops which had spirited out as the blows were struck. I shall never forget that terrible morning, and sometimes I awake with a horrible choking sensation and think that I have just renewed the sickening experience of that day.

"Well, I immediately suspected that the murder had been committed to enable the murderer to rob the bank. I knew that George had no enemies who would seek his life, and there could be no other object in killing him inside the bank."

Mr. Gordon told Pinkerton that the outer door of the vault was standing open, and before he had looked to see what was stolen, he'd checked to make sure George was indeed dead. "His body was cold," he explained. "I sent my clerk to get the sheriff and the coroner. After he ran out [of] the building, another teller and I inspected the vault. I found the keys in the lock of the inner door, and on opening the latter, we saw that everything inside was in great confusion.

"Without making any examination, I closed and locked both doors, and sealed the keyholes with tape and sealing wax. I determined to leave everything just as it was until the inquest should be held. The sheriff and coroner soon arrived and a coroner's jury was impaneled immediately, as, by that time, the news had spread all over town, and the bank was surrounded by nearly all the best men in the place. In summoning the jury, the coroner put down for foreman the name of Mr. Drysdale, George's most intimate friend, but it was found that he was not in the crowd outside, and when they sent for him, he begged so hard to be excused that he was let off."

Mr. Gordon fought back tears as he continued. Pinkerton was sensitive of his feelings but needed to know more about where the body had been found, and what else was around George's remains. Mr. Gordon remembered that a $100 bill from the Planters' Bank of Georgia was clutched tightly in George's hand. George had fallen on his hand when he was hit, and the murderer must have missed it. Mr. Gordon turned the bill bank note stained with blood over to Pinkerton.

Pinkerton learned more from McGregor about clues left behind that might be of significance. Something had been burned in the fireplace. Clothes were suspected, because several buttons were found among the ashes. A charred, twisted piece of paper was also found. Pinkerton inspected the paper, which proved to be a fragment of a bill for $927.78. The signature and part of the date could be read as well. The signature was that of Alexander Drysdale.

There was no question in Pinkerton's mind that county clerk Drysdale was George Gordon's murderer, but the only evidence he had against him was circumstantial. Bank executives wanted the culprit apprehended, but just as importantly, they wanted to recover the stolen $130,000. Pinkerton devised a plan to remedy both problems.

At first the bank executives were reluctant to go along with Pinkerton's scheme, but eventually they acquiesced. To implement his plan, Pinkerton called not only on Kate Warne, but also Timothy Webster, and a third operative named Green. Playing the part of a businessman from Baltimore named John Andrews, Timothy arrived at Atkinson a week prior to Kate, and led those who met him to think he was rich and interested in expanding his holdings in Mississippi. He registered as a guest at the same hotel with Kate, and was regarded by the other patrons at the establishment as a man of great importance and influence.

Posing as Mrs. R. C. Potter, Kate made fast friends with her fellow lodgers. It was through one of these lodgers that she met Alexander Drysdale's wife. Mrs. Drysdale was kind, but seemed sad to Mrs. Potter. She asked her friends if Mrs. Drysdale was feeling well and was told that the woman was preoccupied with worry over her husband. It seemed that Mr. Drysdale had become withdrawn and deeply troubled in a short period of time. Some speculated that he was having financial difficulties, and others believed his problems stemmed from an overwhelming sense of grief. George Gordon's death had so affected him that he couldn't even attend his funeral.

It wasn't until Alexander made the acquaintance of John Andrews that his peculiarities lessened. When Alexander learned that John was interested in investing in land in the area, he invited him to visit his plantation. Alexander hoped to persuade John to purchase the property next to his. He was of the opinion that if John bought the struggling estate, the two could combine their efforts to improve the land and increase the value of the individual parcels.

The two men enjoyed a pleasant ride to the plantation. Timothy Webster reported to Pinkerton that Alexander was "a man of fine education, and fascinating manners, who, for reasons not made known to his loved ones, was disappointed, sour, and morose." By the time the pair had reached Alexander's home, they had become well acquainted and agreed to go hunting the following day.

The scenery around the Drysdales' sprawling house was bold and picturesque. The road they traveled passed through heavy moss-covered timber at times, crossing many ravines and rocky gorges as it followed the general direction of the winding stream. After a pleasant night's sleep, John and Alexander set off on their hunting trip. Game was plentiful, and the two were so preoccupied with the success of their venture that they lost track of time. It was dusk when they started back to the Drysdale plantation, and the mists of night began to form and spread over the landscape. John rode ahead of Alexander. Both were too tired to talk about the day's activities. Suddenly Alexander stopped his horse and let out a gasp. John rode back to find out what was wrong. All the color was gone from Alexander's face; he was trembling violently and could barely speak. When he finally found his voice, all he could say was "Look there."

Pinkerton's report of what transpired that night noted that John found Alexander extremely frightened and nervous. According to John, "His lips were ashy," Pinkerton wrote, "and he had a convulsive grasp on the reins of the horse." He was pointing at something in the near distance. "It was a figure of a young man walking through the timbers, turning his eyes neither to the left or the right," Pinkerton recorded. "He [the young man] was apparently twenty-five or twenty-six years of age. He wore a business suit of light gray clothes, but he had no hat on his head and his curly hair was tossed lightly by the breeze. And when he passed through a clearing and the light from a rising full moon shone on him, it seemed he was more ghost than man. As he moved farther along, the back of his head was more directly exposed and presented a ghastly site [sic]. The thick brown locks were matted together in a mass of gore, and large drops of blood slowly trickled down upon his coat; the whole back of his skull seemed to be crushed in, while the deadly pallor of his face gave him the appearance of a corpse."

Alexander called out to the apparition but the figure continued on its course. John asked him who he was speaking to, and Alexander pointed toward the timber. When John informed Alexander that there was no one there, he became frantic. John tried to convince him that the moonlight must have been playing tricks on him. Alexander was convinced he'd seen a ghost. He made John promise not to mention the incident to his wife.

Mrs. Drysdale could see that her husband was upset when the pair returned to the plantation. Alexander explained that he wasn't feeling well and needed to go to bed. He stayed alone in his room for days. His wife offered to call for a doctor, but he refused to see anyone.

After several days, Alexander emerged from hiding and agreed to spend time again with John. He had taken up drinking and looked haggard, but would not confide in his wife or John the source of his distress. It wasn't until Mrs. Potter was thrown from her horse and the Drysdales came to her rescue that Alexander was distracted enough to focus on something other than his own problems.

Mrs. Potter's room at the Drysdales' home was next to her hosts'. One morning she overheard an interesting conversation which she included in her report to Pinkerton. The couple had awakened at seven in the morning, and Alexander opened the curtains. Shortly after that he let out a sharp cry and fell into a chair. Mrs. Drysdale was at his side in a moment to find out what had happened. He reluctantly admitted to not feeling well. His wife shared with him that she wasn't surprised, because he'd been plagued with a terrible nosebleed overnight. Blood had been found on the sheets and pillows and on the floor leading out the bedroom door, downstairs, out the front door, and all the way out the front gate.

Before Mrs. Drysdale left the bedroom to tend to her household chores, she encouraged Alexander to go back to bed and get more rest. Mrs. Potter heard him pacing and muttering loudly to himself. "This is horrible," she heard him say. "What does this mean? My God! What could have done it?"

John managed to coax Alexander from his room, and the two took a stroll around the grounds. When John pointed out the blood on the grass and on the gate, Alexander claimed the blood must have been from an injured hired hand.

Several days passed before Alexander had another ghostly sighting. This time he and John were joined by two other residents as they rode through the Atkinson countryside around the Drysdale plantation. The ghostly object Alexander referred to as the image of the murdered George Gordon appeared near the same spot as before. Although one of the men agreed he might have witnessed something moving, neither John nor the other riders could claim to have seen an apparition. Alexander nearly collapsed and had to be supported on either side by his friends in order to make it back to his home. He was then confined to his room, too sick to receive visitors.

Pinkerton was made aware of Alexander's condition and advised his operatives to continue their work. He was determined to drive George's killer to confess all.

Less than a week after Alexander had seen the ghost a second time, Mrs. Potter decided to help the land baron's anxiety along. About one o'clock in the morning she arose, quietly dressed, and stealthily left the house. She walked to a nearby creek and began dropping blood from a bottle along the path to the house. She splattered drops up the front walk, in the hall, and finally slipped into Alexander's room and sprinkled drops on his pillow.

When Alexander saw the blood the following morning, he was panic-stricken. Neighbors and hired hands who discovered the bloodstains leading to the house were horrified. Some believed the blood was from a would-be thief whose plans had been thwarted when he'd cut himself somehow, and others believed the blood belonged to an animal that was hurt and trying to find help; still others thought a ghost was somehow responsible.

A few nights later Mrs. Potter caught Alexander sneaking out of the house and following a fresh trail of blood planted by her to the creek. She watched as he waded into the creek and leaned over with his hands in the water as if he were feeling for something. Satisfied that whatever he was hoping to find was there, he walked out of the creek and returned home.

Alexander's health was much improved the following morning, and within a few days he was able to go back to work. Mrs. Potter and an operative named Green who was portraying the ghost of the slain George Gordon monitored Alexander's nighttime activities, which included regular visits to the creek. The detectives were perplexed but didn't waver in their duties. The situation was getting desperate. Mrs. Potter could only feign injury for so long. Eventually she would be compelled to leave the Drysdales' home to return to the hotel.

One late afternoon she agreed to go for a short walk with Mrs. Drysdale, Alexander, and John. She pretended not to be able to keep up with everyone because her legs were stiff. Mrs. Drysdale stayed behind with her while the men kept up a brisk pace in the direction of the creek. Alexander hesitated at first; it was twilight, and he was getting nervous. John continued, undeterred. He was watching a hawk passing overhead when Alexander gasped and dropped to his knees. Crossing the path on the opposite side of the creek was the terrible specter he had seen twice before. It moved out of sight quickly. Alexander fainted. John called for help, and Mrs. Drysdale hurried to her husband. Mrs. Potter hobbled to the scene as the hired hands rushed in from the fields to assist. Alexander was carried to his house and deposited into his bed.

When Alexander recovered, he was white as a sheet and shaking. John was by his side, and Alexander reached out and grabbed his arm.

"John," he began, "did you see that horrible ghost?"

John shook his head. "No, indeed; I saw no ghost," he told him.

Alexander questioned his wife and Mrs. Potter, and both responded negatively. The terrified man could not accept their answers. John poured him a glass of brandy, and Alexander drank it down, trying to make sense of what had happened. Mrs. Drysdale burst into tears and pleaded with her husband to let them take him to a reliable physician. Alexander would not agree, and demanded to be left alone.

Operative Green kept a careful eye on the house that evening. Mrs. Potter and John brought him food and instructed him to wait in the woods until the following morning. In the middle of the night, Green observed the door of the Drysdales' home open and Alexander step out. Wearing only his dressing robe, he wandered about like someone walking in his sleep. He didn't stay outside long; after roaming around a bit, he returned inside.

The next evening Alexander behaved in much the same way, but this time he traveled to the creek. Green watched him closely as he bent down and searched in the water for something. Once it seemed he'd found it, he marked the area by placing a stone on the bank of the creek. Alexander then hurried back to the house.

Green wasted no time in getting to the spot where Alexander had been standing in the water.

During Alexander's absence, Mrs. Potter had snuck into his room and sprinkled drops of blood on his pillow and on the floor around the bed. She managed to get out of his room just as he entered the home. She observed him going back to his room and shutting the door behind him. Mrs. Potter peered through the keyhole to see what he did next. She watched as he tried to wash the bloodstains off the floor.

Alexander was in poor health by this point, both physically and emotionally. He wouldn't get out of bed and refused to eat. He sent for John and asked him to retrieve paperwork from his office in Atkinson and bring it to him. John agreed. Using the key Alexander gave him, he gained access to his private office. Before leaving with the documents, John scattered drops of blood about the room. He raced back to the Drysdales' plantation with the documents. When Alexander inquired if he'd had any problems, John informed him about the blood on the chairs, desk, and paperwork. As he spoke he held out the documents dotted with crimson stains. The shock proved too much for Alexander, and he fainted. It was some time before he came to.

While Alexander lay struggling with all he had experienced, John conspired with bank executives to sprinkle blood in the bank on the floor and desk where George used to work. The plan was set in motion. Bank employees who discovered the blood were shaken by the sight. When news of the discovery reached Alexander, his nerves became even more raw. John told Pinkerton that Alexander was like a man suffering from hydrophobia more commonly known as rabies. "His thoughts could turn in only one direction," the operative explained, "and that was toward remorse and fear." John conveyed to the operatives he was working with that things were approaching a crisis level.

A doctor was called to the Drysdales' home, and after examining the patient, he prescribed a healthy dosage of morphine to make Alexander sleep. The doctor was fairly certain that once the disturbed man fell asleep, he would stay asleep for several hours.

John seized the opportunity to gather his crew and the bank executives to explore the creek area on which Alexander had been so fixated. Green stayed behind, dressed as the murder victim, ready to scare Alexander should he wake up unexpectedly and decide to venture to the water again.

At midnight under a fair, moonlit sky, John and the three bank executives converged at the creek bed. They had no sooner started toward the marked spot in the water when Green came running at them. Alexander was up and out of his bed and heading their way. Green walked in front of Alexander as George a couple of times, but Drysdale didn't act like he saw George at all.

John and the others hid in the brush and waited for Alexander to come near. John studied the man's actions and determined that Alexander was sleepwalking. His anxiety and nervous dread was so great that he couldn't rest in quiet, and was driven to visit the spot where he'd hidden the blood-stained treasure he'd stolen.

Alexander waded into the creek and began splashing in the water frantically. Unable to locate the object he was compelled to collect, he shuffled back to his home. Once he was out of sight, John took up the search. Using a pickax and shovel, he dug into the creek bed until he struck a hollow piece of wood. The bank executives flanked him on either side and assisted in removing the log. Once the log was out of the way they unearthed a large, heavy metal box. Inside were the gold coins that had been taken. The bundles of cash were not in the box. John assured the bank executives that he would have the remainder of the money returned to them in twenty-four hours.

—◆—

Alexander was grateful that John came to visit him the following day. The frazzled man was not willing to let him out of his sight for a moment. John's presence was a welcome distraction to Alexander. The time the two of them spent talking about hunting, fishing, or horseback riding were the only moments Alexander wasn't thinking about the crime he had committed. It wasn't until late in the evening when Alexander had drifted asleep during a conversation that John had a chance to break away. He crept outside and walked to a grove of trees beyond the garden to rendezvous with Green and Mrs. Potter. Green had witnessed Alexander wandering around the grove one evening and suspected the money might have been buried there.

Armed with lanterns, the three examined the ground in search of loose sod. They did find a patch of fresh earth that seemed suspicious, and John dug beneath it. At a depth of two feet, they came upon a large candle-box which they carefully extracted from the ground with a shovel. The spot was immediately covered over again with dirt and patted down in order to remove any evidence that someone had been there. John took the box to the bank in Atkinson, Green returned to his post watching the house, and Mrs. Potter made her way to Alexander's room, splattering blood along the path as she went.

At daylight the bank executives opened the box and discovered the stolen cash. John watched as the money was carried to the vault and locked inside. By the time John returned to the Drysdale plantation, Alexander was sick with fear and convulsing. The bloodstains on the floor and his bed had driven him close to madness. John reported to Pinkerton that Alexander's terror was "greater than he had ever shown before."

Pinkerton and his operatives were convinced of Alexander's guilt, but still had no legal evidence sufficient enough to convict him, in case he should maintain his innocence. Pinkerton's concerns were not limited to the circumstantial evidence. "I had assumed a terrible responsibility in taking such extreme measures with him," he noted in the case file, "for there was danger that he might go insane without confessing his guilt. In that case my position would have been really dangerous. I should have been accused of giving the orders to drive him crazy with no proper justification for my actions, and the result might have been most disastrous to me. The fact that I, an unknown man from the North, had helped drive a high-toned Southern gentleman insane would have been sufficient to hang me by the summary process of lynch law."

Pinkerton met again with his operatives, and they further outlined the problems of a case without a full confession. A lawyer could argue that it could not be proven that Alexander buried the money on his property. Nor could it be proven that he was driven to the area where the money was located out of guilt over his actions. Mrs. Potter reminded Pinkerton that Alexander was a sleepwalker, and suggested that perhaps he was sleepwalking the night George was murdered. She suggested that Alexander could have simply followed the murderer to the spot where the gold was hidden.

Pinkerton learned the Drysdales had decided to sell their property in Atkinson and move to New Orleans. The troubled couple was in agreement that starting over in a new location might improve Alexander's health. Mrs. Drysdale made plans for her husband to go to his office to close their accounts. When Pinkerton discovered the Drysdales' intentions, he drew up the necessary affidavit to have Alexander arrested. John accompanied an unsuspecting Alexander to his office. They had no sooner arrived when the sheriff entered the business and presented the warrant to Alexander. He was taken aback and demanded to know why he was being arrested. When the officer told him it was for the murder of George Gordon, Alexander let out a scream and fainted. John assisted in reviving the accused, and law enforcement asked the two men to go to the bank with them.

It was twilight when the sheriff, Alexander, and John journeyed down the street to the bank. Pinkerton met them at the door, introduced himself, and reinforced that Alexander was to be taken into custody for murder.

"Have you any denial to make?" Pinkerton asked.

Before he could respond, operative Green passed behind George Gordon's desk and stood in the spot where the man was killed. As on previous occasions, Alexander turned white as a sheet and collapsed. Restoratives were applied, and he soon recovered. No one but Alexander claimed to see the ghost, and it made him frantic. He denied the charges made against him and called them "false in every particular way."

Pinkerton placed a box on top of one of the desks and then asked the crazed man if he also denied he had buried gold in the creek. Pinkerton opened the box and removed a few sacks of gold. Alexander said nothing. He merely hung his head and drew in a long breath. "Will you also deny that you buried the paper money in a grave near your home on the plantation?" Pinkerton expounded on the evidence, telling the accused about the partially burned notes and buttons found in the fire. Alexander sat stone-faced, either not knowing how to respond or too afraid to speak.

According to the file Pinkerton maintained on the case, his next move was a desperate one.

"If you're not satisfied with the evidence that we can prove you are guilty," Pinkerton told Alexander, "I will call upon the murdered man himself to testify against you."

As Pinkerton spoke, Green slowly reappeared behind the desk.

Alexander covered his face with his hands and dropped to his knees. "Oh! My God! I am guilty!! I am guilty!!" he cried out. Once Alexander began confessing, he couldn't stop. He told every detail of the crime except for why. He had no answer to that question. "I've not known a moment's peace since then," he cried. "My mind has been occupied with that money constantly, and even in my sleep I would dream about it."

The more Alexander talked, the more the motive for the murder became clear. He was going broke and couldn't pay his debts. One of the debtors was pressuring him, and he was becoming more desperate. He had removed the $300 he had left in his account and applied for a loan from the bank for the rest. While George Gordon had been counting out the cash to give to Alexander, he struck him with a hammer, stole the money from the vault, and buried it.

Alexander seemed resigned to the fact that he was going to jail, and asked the sheriff for a moment alone to write a note to his wife. The sheriff agreed. Alexander requested that John be allowed to go with him into one of the bank executives' offices while he penned the letter. That request was also approved. Alexander wanted John to take the letter to his wife.

The two men stepped into the office, and John helped Alexander to a desk. Alexander grabbed his hand and held it tightly. "Tell my wife I feel better for having confessed," he implored the operative. John nodded and handed him a piece of paper. As he turned away to close the door behind them, Alexander removed a pistol from his jacket pocket and shot himself in the head.

Mrs. Potter was at Mrs. Drysdale's side when she was informed of her husband's arrest and subsequent death.

NOTES
1. Pinkerton, *The Detective and the Somnambulist; The Murderer and the Fortune Teller*, pp. 3–101; "Jane Maxwell Drysdale" (www.ancestry.com/genealogy/records/jane -maxwell-drysdale_45857219).

CHAPTER THREE

OPERATIVE HATTIE LEWIS LAWTON

AN ARTICLE IN THE MAY 14, 1893, EDITION OF THE *NEW YORK TIMES* categorized women as the "weaker, gentler sex whose special duty was the creation of an orderly and harmonious sphere for husbands and children. Respectable women, true women, do not participate in debates on the public issues or attract attention to themselves."[1] Kate Warne and the female operatives who served with her defied convention, and progressive men like Allan Pinkerton gave them an opportunity to prove themselves capable of more than caring for a home and family.

Kate's daring and Pinkerton's ingenuity paved the way for women to be accepted in the field of law enforcement. Prior to Kate being hired as an agent, few had been given a chance to serve as female officers in any capacity.

In the early 1840s, six women were put in charge of female inmates at a prison in New York. Their appointments led to a handful of other ladies being allowed to patrol dance halls, skating rinks, pool halls, movie theaters, and other places of amusement frequented by women and children. Although the patrol women performed their duties admirably, local government officials and police departments were reluctant to issue them uniforms or allow them to carry weapons. The general consensus among men was that women lacked the physical stamina to maintain such a job for an extended period of time.[2] An article in an 1859 edition of *The Citizen* newspaper announced that "Women are the fairer sex, unable to reason rationally or withstand trauma. They depend upon the protection of men."[3]

The Woman's Christian Temperance Union played a key role in helping to change the stereotypical view of women at the time. The organization recognized the treatment female convicts suffered in prison and campaigned for women to be put in charge of female inmates. The WCTU's efforts were successful. Prison matrons provided assistance and direction to female prisoners, thereby shielding them from possible abuse at the hands of male officers and inmates. Those matrons were the earliest predecessors of women law enforcement officers.[4]

Aside from women hired specifically as police matrons, widows of slain police officers were sometimes given honorary positions within the department. Titles given to widows meant little at the time; it was, however, the first hint of what would eventually lead to official positions for sworn-in policewomen.[5]

Even with their limited duties, police matrons in the mid- to late 1800s suffered a barrage of negative publicity. Most of the commentary scoffed at the women's infiltration into the field. The press approached stories about police matrons and other women trying to force their way into the trade as "confused or cute," rather than a useful addition to the law enforcement community.[6]

Allan Pinkerton's decision to hire a female operative was all the more courageous given the public's perception of women as law enforcement agents. Kate Warne had the foresight to know that she could be especially helpful in cases where male operatives needed to collect evidence from female suspects. She quickly proved to be a valuable asset, and Pinkerton hoped Hattie Lewis, also known as Hattie Lawton, would be just as effective.[7] Hired in 1860, not only was Hattie the second woman employed at the world-famous detective agency, but some historians speculate she was also the first mixed-race woman as well.[8]

Pinkerton was an exceptional man, looking beyond gender and race as few did at the time. In the late 1840s, he was active in the Underground Railroad, helping many runaway slaves escape to Canada. He spoke out against the Fugitive Slave Act passed by the US Congress in September 1850. The law penalized officials who did not arrest an alleged runaway slave, and subjected them to a fine of $1,000 for aiding any fugitive in his or her efforts to be free. Since any suspected slave was not eligible for a trial, the law resulted in the kidnapping and conscription of free blacks into slavery, as suspected fugitive slaves had no rights in court and could not defend themselves against accusations.[9]

Chicago became a clearinghouse for runaway slaves. In rural areas such as Dundee, where Pinkerton resided, some enterprising young men were forming businesses to hunt fugitive slaves for a reward. Pinkerton was outraged by the "bloodhounds," and sought ways to defy them. In 1857, he was one of a delegation called to investigate a slave catcher passing through town. Historians believe it was during this investigation that he met Hattie Lawton. Some of Hattie's family was suspected of being among a party of slaves Pinkerton was sheltering as they prepared to disperse to Canada.[10]

Born in 1837, Pinkerton described the widowed Hattie as "delicate and driven." He wrote that "her complexion was fresh and rose-like in the morning. Her hair fell in flowing tresses. She appeared careless and entirely at ease, but a close observer would have noticed a compression of the small lips, and a fixedness in the sparkling eyes that told of a purpose to be accomplished."[11]

Hattie played a key role at the detective agency for many years, assuming various identities and ferreting out information that aided in solving numerous cases. One of the most dangerous assignments in which Hattie participated involved gathering intelligence about Confederate Army movements. In 1862, Hattie and Pinkerton operative Timothy Webster were dispatched to Richmond, Virginia, posing as a wealthy married couple.[12]

Allan Pinkerton was working with General George B. McClellan, who was general in chief of the Union Army. Pinkerton would become the officer's personal secret operative. General McClellan received orders from the president at the White House, and he passed them along to Pinkerton, who passed them on to the operatives in the field. Hattie and Timothy pretended to be Rebel sympathizers from Perrymansville, Maryland. Timothy had indeed been in Perrymansville, working to expose a suspected plot by malcontents to damage railroad property.

Then, all of the sudden, the situation became of national importance, and for a time Pinkerton and Timothy were part of history in the making.[13]

Just prior to relocating to Virginia, Timothy had been living in Baltimore and working on cases for the detective agency. His primary objective was to gain acceptance from groups of Southern sympathizers in the area and find out their plans to thwart the Union's military efforts. After several months, Timothy managed to infiltrate a secessionist group known as the Sons of Liberty. The Sons of Liberty was an underground organization determined to help overtake the government, and Timothy became one of their most trusted members. Confederate secretary of war Judah P. Benjamin recruited him to be a courier for the Confederates' "secret line" between Washington, Baltimore, and Richmond. The Pinkerton operative ensured that the documents he was carrying made it not only to Rebel combatants, but also to Union officers and Pinkerton staff members. His relationship with the Sons of Liberty was to continue after he relocated.

Unfortunately, the detective fell prey to inflammatory rheumatism and was unable to deliver messages to and from Confederate spies. Daily reports to Pinkerton had stopped as well. Fortunately for the detective agency, another operative was ready to take over Timothy's duties.[14]

Hattie Lawton and Timothy Webster were living at the Monument Hotel in Richmond, Virginia, when he became sick. The numerous trips Timothy made across the Potomac River in frigid weather to transport secret documents back and forth brought on his illness. He was confined to bed, and Hattie was by his side to nurse him. She did not have the relationships he did to carry on with his responsibilities as a courier, but she was determined to find her own way to gain secrets.[15]

Hattie was well acquainted with Confederate secretary of war Benjamin and many members of his staff. They would tip their hats to her on the street and ask about her husband. She believed she could acquire information from one or all of the war cabinet in a social setting; perhaps at a dinner the men might discuss details between one another that could be overheard.[16]

In late February 1862, Hattie recruited the help of a Pinkerton operative living in Washington named John Scobell. John had been working for the detective agency since the fall of 1861. He was a former slave in

Mississippi who had been well educated by his owner, a Scotsman, who had freed him. According to the Central Intelligence archives, he was quick-witted and an accomplished role player, allowing him to function in several different capacities on various missions, including as a cook, laborer, and a musician. He often worked with Pinkerton agents, sometimes playing the role of a servant who attended to horses.

Hattie wanted John to pose as the Websters' servant and eavesdrop on influential Southern contacts when she and Timothy socialized. In between such engagements, John planned to visit popular taverns in the area to sing and pass the hat. He hoped he might pick up information from Southerners in these settings. After two weeks he learned that Confederate general Joseph E. Johnston was escorting three regiments of Rebel soldiers to Yorktown.[17]

"Good God!" Hattie remarked when John shared the news. "That means a whole army corps is moving, at least twenty thousand men." John drafted a report to Pinkerton, and Hattie hurried to tell her superior, Kate Warne, also in Richmond at the time, what had been revealed.[18]

In the weeks that followed, John and Hattie rode out to the Confederate fortifications surrounding Richmond nearly every afternoon. She was welcomed everywhere. "A pretty young woman was always a cheering sight for battle-fatigued soldiers," Pinkerton noted in his own report about the matter years later. While Hattie chatted with officers, John, unnoticed, would inventory everything in sight and sketch the entrenchments at will. His daily reports were lengthy. More and more, Hattie was serving as a distraction while John performed the real espionage.[19]

The majority of orders the spies received from Pinkerton in Washington were addressed to both Hattie and John, but on occasion a message would come through solely for John to read. Those messages would be stuffed into the barrel of a revolver. Not long after the pair had sent word to Pinkerton about Rebel troop movements, a message was delivered to John concealed in a gun. The coded message John deciphered read: "McClellan ready to move. No time for sending reports through here. Daily reports must go directly to McClellan. Find a way through lines so Mrs. Lawton can hand reports to Captain Lawton. Extremely important and dangerous. Always be armed. You must protect Mrs. Lawton at any cost. Pinkerton."[20]

The following morning John told Hattie about Pinkerton's message. When night fell, the operatives rode out into the country. Outside Richmond, they waited until the sun rose the next day before pressing on. Hattie had a pass to ride through the lines by day, but the pass was not good in the evenings. They had been instructed by Pinkerton to meet Captain Lawton at an intersection in front of a church. Both knew the location, and at the appointed time the three converged at the rendezvous point.

The first meeting was brief, as Captain Lawton feared they might be discovered. He asked that Hattie and John meet him at an inn in Glendale, farther away from their initial rendezvous site. He believed they could meet there regularly and safely. The inn was run by a woman supposedly loyal to the Union. Daily reports intended for General McClellan and compiled by the spies were hidden in the hollow handle of Hattie's riding crop. John, acting as her groom (a servant who attends to the horses), rode with a Smith & Wesson tucked inside his shirt. He vowed to protect Hattie, just as Pinkerton had advised.[21]

During one of the exchanges of reports, John noticed a certain peddler acting suspiciously. The traveling salesman was too loud and overly friendly with the patrons. His backslapping camaraderie was too exaggerated to be sincere. He bought too many drinks for too many people. John shared with Hattie and the captain his concern that the peddler might be a counterspy. The captain left the inn immediately, hoping the cagey man would follow him.[22]

Sensing their conversation had been compromised, Hattie and John decided they needed to return to McClellan's headquarters and arrange for transportation back to Washington. Hattie believed if they didn't return to Pinkerton's office at the capitol, they risked being arrested by the Rebels and hanged. Timothy continued to struggle with his health, but she and John agreed that his safety, as well as their own, was paramount.[23]

Just as the spies were about to leave the inn, a stable boy stopped John to let him know that the peddler who had set out after the captain had backtracked and was now waiting down the road with four armed riders. John reasoned the counterspy was guarding against their possible escape to McClellan's headquarters.[24]

According to Pinkerton's account of the spies' experience as relayed to him in their reports, both were well armed and fully prepared to defend themselves. John stressed to Hattie that their horses were superior to the mounts the peddler and his men had. If they managed to sneak out of the inn, they could ride hard to the nearest Union garrison, twenty miles away. "If we get into trouble," John reportedly told Hattie, "I'm going to shoot it out, but you keep going. You and Allan Pinkerton are more important than any one man."[25]

The pair left the inn through a side door and rode swiftly along at a free and sweeping gallop. Their horses were steady, fast, and sure. They were able to put a great deal of distance between themselves and the inn, and in a short time felt a bit more at ease. "I guess we will get through all right, notwithstanding our fears to the contrary," Hattie remarked to John. "I don't know about that," John replied. "We're not through with our journey, and there's plenty of time for trouble yet. Perhaps we had better walk the horses a spell."[26]

The pair dismounted and led their rides through a richly cultivated district; on either side were farms whose growing crops had not yet been touched by the ravages of war, and the country, under the soft light of the moon, presented a scene of rare beauty. To the left ran the James River; to the right, the country was broken and hilly. The night was soft and balmy, the silence only broken by the sound of the horses' hooves as they slowly trotted along. Once the spies felt the horses were sufficiently rested, they climbed back into their saddles and quickly pressed forward to a spot called Wilcox's Wharf, just beyond which was the Union garrison.[27]

As the pair approached a growth of timber through which they had to ride, an instinctive feeling of dread came over both of them. "Just the place for an ambush," Hattie said. "Draw your pistol, John, and be ready in case of an attack." He did as suggested and urged his horse ahead of Hattie's. The two made it safely to the edge of the woods, but as they emerged on the other side the peddler and his riders were waiting.

"What to do now was a question to be decided promptly," Pinkerton later wrote of the incident. "To turn and retreat would certainly ensure their capture . . . so they resolved to bravely continue on their way. A few hurried words were exchanged between them, as they arranged that each should select a man and fire on him the instant they were challenged."[28]

As the riders approached, the spies were divided, two going on each side of the road, leaving a space between them. Two of the riders were wearing Confederate uniforms, and two were dressed in civilian clothes. All were heavily armed. The peddler let out a Rebel yell, and Hattie and John spurred their horses into a full gallop. The men hurried after them and in a matter of minutes gradually closed in on the pair. John had his revolver in his hand, but wouldn't fire on the group until he was sure he would hit one of them.[29]

The road the spies and counterspies raced down suddenly curved, and the full moon drifted behind the clouds, leaving the pathway in the shadows. John's horse stepped into a hole, stumbled, and fell. He was thrown unharmed from his mount. Hattie jerked her horse to a stop, turned the animal around, and raced back to the spot where John had hit the ground. He scrambled to his feet and waved to Hattie before she had a chance to climb out of the saddle.

"Are you hurt?" she asked.

"No, but my horse is," he replied. "Go ahead. Don't mind me," he ordered. "Save yourself." She heard the Rebels yell again and sped off in the direction of the Union camp.[30]

Listening intently, John could hear the clatter of the hooves of Hattie's horse in the near distance. Coming closer every instant was the sound of the approaching horsemen. John urged his injured horse to the side of the road and placed himself behind the animal; resting his weapon across the saddle, he waited for the approaching horsemen. The Confederate riders were nearly upon John, who knew he made a good target in the moonlight. When the first rider's horse was almost on top of him, John took careful aim and fired his gun. The horse went down with a bullet through its head. The rider was knocked unconscious. John shot and killed the second rider. He emptied the remaining rounds into a third Rebel, who uttered a scream of anguish and toppled from the saddle.[31]

John ducked down to quickly reload his weapon. The remaining man stopped his horse with a jerk that drew the animal back upon his haunches, and then, turning the horse swiftly around, set off in the opposite direction, back toward Richmond. John fired at him as he rode away.[32]

It wasn't long before John heard hoofbeats coming from the direction of the path Hattie had taken. In a moment the operative was surrounded by members of the US Cavalry, commanded by Captain Lawton and led by Hattie. John informed the captain that the fourth rider had fled, and a party of four was ordered to track down the renegade. The soldiers soon found the rider lying dead in the bush. The last bullet John had fired had struck the man—who turned out to be the peddler—in the arm, shattering it. The deceased man was taken to the Union lines.[33]

John was sent to Pinkerton's headquarters in Washington and reassigned to another case. Hattie returned to Webster's sickbed to continue caring for him.

It was subsequently learned that the peddler was a Rebel spy who for some time had been visiting the Union camps, gathering information, which he no doubt conveyed to other Confederates. "On his person were found papers which fully confirmed this," Pinkerton later wrote about the case. "That they failed to reach their destination was a fortunate occurrence for the Union cause."[34]

Despite Hattie's round-the-clock nursing, Timothy Webster's health continued to decline. He was in constant pain, and his joints and muscles were grotesquely swollen. His rheumatism was so far advanced that he had trouble walking and feeding himself. Hattie focused all of her attention on him. Reports to Pinkerton from the two operatives were few and far between. Concerned for the safety of the pair, Pinkerton sent detectives John Scully and Pryce Lewis to investigate.[35]

The Monument Hotel where Timothy and Hattie were living was a popular hostelry for statesmen, military leaders, and politicians. Spies and counterspies from both the North and South frequented the halls and lobby of the establishment, exchanging secrets and quietly discussing battle plans. Operatives John Scully and Pryce Lewis were unaware that Confederate agents had tailed them from Washington to Richmond. The Pinkerton men were followed to the hotel and to the Websters' room. As they were leaving, they were recognized by a Rebel soldier, Lieutenant

Chase Morton. Scully and Lewis had arrested Lieutenant Morton's Southern-sympathizing father, Senator Jackson Morton, in late 1861. The lieutenant had the operatives taken into custody and charged with espionage. Neither Timothy nor Hattie was arrested, but a blanket of suspicion covered their every move.[36]

Scully and Lewis were tried, convicted, and sentenced to be hanged on April 4, 1862. They were granted stays of execution when it was revealed that both men were not American citizens but British subjects. Attorneys for the operatives advised their clients that the order to hang them could be reinstituted if they didn't cooperate with the Confederate Army and tell all they knew. Pryce Lewis steadfastly refused to give the Rebel leaders any information. John Scully, however, was intimidated into giving up names of double agents, one of whom was Timothy Webster.[37]

The accusations against Timothy were dismissed at first because he was so well connected with Confederate officials, who didn't believe Timothy was capable of being a counterspy. Only after Scully had cited examples of Timothy's duplicity did the Rebel leaders believe the operative was telling the truth. As a result of Scully's willingness to share, both his and Lewis's death sentences were commuted. Erroneous information spread that Lewis, as well as Scully, had betrayed Timothy. The error was compounded later when Hattie reported the betrayal as well. Pryce Lewis fought hard to clear his name; the stigma of his betrayal hounded him for most of his life. Neither John Scully nor Pryce Lewis would work for Pinkerton again. In 1911 Lewis ended his life by jumping off the dome of the World Building in New York.[38]

If Timothy's health had been better, no doubt he and Hattie would have attempted to flee Richmond. Timothy tried to convince Hattie to leave and save herself, but she refused. Several days of anxious suspense followed before they were arrested by Confederate authorities and taken to a jail called Castle Godwin in Richmond. The Castle was a converted tobacco warehouse, and most often referred to as a hellhole. George Alexander was the cruel prison superintendent.[39]

Allan Pinkerton's official report to President Lincoln, General McClellan, and the provost marshal general about agents Timothy Webster and Hattie Lawton noted that the atmosphere inside the prison was gloomy and reeked of filth and disease. When Timothy was initially led into the dank, dark prison, he could hardly walk. He was pale and emaciated. The inmates pitied him and feared the next step would be to intern the dead man at the jail along with the living.[40]

Hattie was taken by guards to Confederate officers for questioning, but she refused to answer a single query. Her stubbornness infuriated the officers, and they ordered her to be confined in a room with another female prisoner.[41]

Fearing that Timothy would die before his trial, the provost marshal called for investigators to quickly prepare the case against the operative. Court was convened for early afternoon the day after Timothy and Hattie had been arrested, and was initially held at the jail. "For three long, weary weeks did the investigation drag its slow length along," Pinkerton wrote about the case, "although it was apparent that those who tried him had already decided upon his fate. Numerous witnesses were examined, and testimony was admitted which would have been excluded by any righteous tribunal whose ideas of justice were not obscured by an insane desire for revenge."

Pryce Lewis and John Scully were called to testify about Timothy's involvement as a double agent. They attempted to do their utmost to lessen the effect of their testimony, but it bore heavily against the ill prisoner. The attorney assigned to represent the accused did the best he could, but could not save the Pinkerton operative from the guilty verdict that was ultimately rendered. On April 19, 1862, Timothy was convicted of being a spy in the employ of the Federal authorities. The judge sentenced him to be hanged, and the execution date was set for April 28, 1862.[42]

The day after Timothy's execution was set, Hattie was given permission to visit him in his cell. The two hadn't been allowed to communicate with one another since the day they'd been arrested. "The meeting between Timothy and Hattie was a most affecting one," Pinkerton noted in the report about the matter. "Tears filled the eyes of the faithful woman as she gazed at the pale and emaciated form of the heroic patriot. Their hands were clasped in a warm pressure, and her words of heartfelt sympathy and grief were choked by the sobs which shook her frame. Even in the excess of his despair, Webster's fortitude never for a moment forsook him. He bore the burdens which had been imposed upon him with courage and firmness that impressed all who witnessed it."[43]

In an effort to make his cell sanitary, Hattie washed the bedding and his clothes and was allowed to cook a meal for him. She wanted Timothy to be made comfortable in his last days. In addition to improving her fellow operative's living conditions, she sought an interview with Confederate president Jefferson Davis. Davis was too busy discussing war with General Lee to speak with Hattie, but Davis's wife agreed to see her. On bended knee Hattie pleaded for Mrs. Davis to intercede to have Timothy's life spared. The woman declined to interfere in matters of state. Crying, Hattie left the Davises' home, utterly discouraged. She vowed to fight to remain by Timothy's side until the day he was to be taken to the gallows.[44]

Timothy petitioned the Confederate court to put him to death by any other means but hanging. Officials visited him in his cell to tell him they would not change the sentence. Hattie was frantic when she heard the news. She was unable to restrain herself and fell at the messengers' feet. "Please," Hattie interjected. "Do not, I pray you, condemn this brave man to the odium of a felon's death. Think of his family and his suffering. He does not sue for pardon. He seeks not to escape your judgment, harsh and cruel as it is. He only prays to be allowed to die like a brave man in the service of his country. You certainly can lose nothing by granting this request; therefore, in the name of justice and humanity, let him be shot instead of the dreadful death you have ordained for him."[45]

Her request was denied; Hattie's plea was for naught. "Then he will die like a man and his death will be upon your head," she called out to the cold, unfeeling officials. "It will be a living curse until your own dark hour shall come!"[46]

At 5:15 in the morning of April 28, 1862, guards unlocked Timothy Webster's cell to escort him to the parade grounds where he was to be hanged. Turning to Hattie and taking her hands in his, Timothy murmured, "Good-bye, dear friend; we shall never meet again on earth. God bless you and your kindness to me. I will be brave and die like a man. Farewell, forever." Hattie wailed and threw herself onto the floor as the guards led Timothy out of his cell.[47]

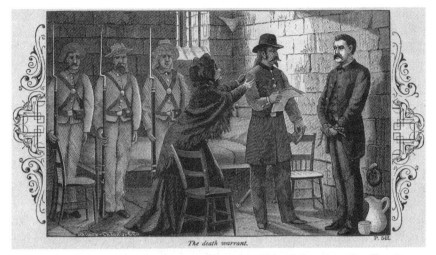

The death warrant. P. 542.

Pinkerton operative Hattie Lawton pleaded for the life of fellow detective Timothy Webster in 1862. COURTESY OF THE LIBRARY OF CONGRESS

The gallows were located at the north side of the parade grounds. Timothy walked unflinchingly to the scaffold, and then slowly and painfully ascended the platform. His arms were tied behind him; his feet were bound together, and a black cap was placed over his head. The signal was given, the trap was sprung, and, with a dreadful, sickening thud, Timothy fell from the gibbet to the ground beneath. The hangman's knot had slipped, and he fell in a confused heap. Timothy was lifted up and returned to the scaffold.[48]

"I suffer a double death," Timothy told the men around him. The rope was again placed around his neck, this time so tightly it was painful. "You will choke me to death this time," the condemned man said. In a flash, the trap was again sprung, and the brave patriot was swinging in the air between heaven and earth.[49]

The captain of the guards returned to Timothy's cell to inform Hattie that her friend was dead. She asked if she could see his body, and the guard led the way. Several Rebel soldiers were standing around the coffin when Hattie entered the room where Timothy was lying in state. Overwrought with despair and angry over the treatment of her partner, Hattie unleashed a torrent of emotion. "Murderers!" she exclaimed to the

Confederate troops and officers on either side of her. "This is your work! If there is vengeance or retribution in this world, you will feel it before you die!"[50]

Hattie petitioned the Rebel court to allow her to bury Timothy in a New York cemetery where he had once been a police officer, but her request was denied. Timothy's body was buried in an obscure corner of a paupers' field, not far from where he was hanged.[51]

Hattie, who had been convicted of being a conspirator of espionage with Timothy, was sentenced to one year in prison. She was often visited by Elizabeth Van Lew, a Southern-born, Union sympathizer who operated from Richmond during the Civil War. Elizabeth brought scraps of food and other comforts to the women and elderly at Castle Godwin. The benevolent woman managed to negotiate Hattie's release from jail on December 13, 1862. Hattie's freedom and that of three other Federals were exchanged for the release of the notorious Rebel spy, Belle Boyd.[52]

Hattie proved herself to be a loyal and valuable member of the Pinkerton force. Her talent in espionage, combined with the skills of the other Pinkerton operatives, helped save the life of President Abraham Lincoln.

NOTES

1. *New York Times*, May 14, 1893.
2. Duffin, *History in Blue*, pp. 1–5.
3. *The Citizen*, 1859.
4. Duffin, *History in Blue*, pp. 3–4.
5. Ibid.
6. *Decatur Morning Review*, September 17, 1890.
7. Sources conflict as to whether Hattie Lawton was the true name of the operative. Many accounts use only her initials, H. H. L. Allan Pinkerton referred to her as Hattie Lawton in his book, *The Spy of the Rebellion*. Pryce Lewis referred to her in his memoirs as Hattie Lewis. In a letter written by Allan Pinkerton to Joseph B. Beale, dated October 26, 1882, he refers to the operative as Hattie Lewis.
8. Moran, *The Eye That Never Sleeps*, pp. 21–23.
9. Fugitive Slave Act, September 18, 1850; Morris, *Ordeal of the Union: Fruits of Manifest Destiny, 1847–1852*, pp. 49–51.
10. Pierce, *A History of Chicago*, p. 198.
11. Stashower, *The Hour of Peril*, pp. 99–101.
12. Horan, *The Pinkertons*, pp. 98–100.
13. Ward et al., *The Civil War*, pp. 76–77; *Washington Post*, February 13, 1913.
14. Pinkerton, *Spy of the Rebellion*, pp. 553–54.

15. Ibid., pp. 496–98.
16. Ibid.
17. Horan, *The Pinkertons*, pp. 103–04; "Black Dispatches: Black American Contributions to Union Intelligence during the Civil War," Central Intelligence Agency (www .cia.gov/library/center-for-the-study-of-intelligence/csi-publications/books-and -monographs/black-dispatches/); *Ebony Magazine* (February 1965, October 1978).
18. *Ebony Magazine* (February 1965, October 1978); Horan, *The Pinkertons*, pp. 103–04; "Black Dispatches."
19. Foster, *The Eyes and Ears of the Civil War*, pp. 116–20.
20. Foster, The Eyes and Ears of the Civil War, pp. 116–20; "Black Dispatches." (*Note:* Author found no information to confirm or deny that Hattie Lawton was married to Captain Lawton.)
21. Pinkerton, *Spy of the Rebellion*, pp. 530–34.
22. Pinkerton, *Spy of the Rebellion*, pp. 530–34; "Black Dispatches."
23. Pinkerton, *Spy of the Rebellion*, pp. 534–42.
24. Ibid.
25. Ibid.
26. Ibid.
27. Ibid.
28. Ibid.
29. Ibid.
30. Ibid.
31. Ibid.
32. Ibid.
33. Ibid.
34. Ibid.
35. Horan, *The Pinkertons*, pp. 109–14.
36. Horan, *The Pinkertons*, pp. 109–14; Jones, *Behind Enemy Lines*, pp. 43–47.
37. Jones, *Behind Enemy Lines*, p. 44; Horan, *The Pinkertons*, pp. 138–39.
38. *New York Times*, December 11, 1911.
39. Horan, *The Pinkertons*, pp. 138–39; *Burlington Daily Hawk Eye*, May 7, 1862.
40. Pinkerton, *Spy of the Rebellion*, pp. 541–50.
41. Ibid.
42. Ibid.
43. Ibid.
44. Ibid.
45. Ibid., pp. 551–56.
46. Ibid.
47. Ibid.
48. Ibid.
49. Ibid.
50. Ibid.
51. Ibid.
52. Ibid.

CHAPTER FOUR

OPERATIVE
MRS. M. BARKLEY

IN FEBRUARY 1861, ALLAN PINKERTON WAS LIVING IN BALTIMORE, Maryland, where, as "John H. Hutchinson, Stockbroker," he was instigating reports of contemplated sabotage on the tracks and property of the Philadelphia, Wilmington and Baltimore Railroad. The PW&B Railroad was one of the most important rail lines at the time. According to the history of the company, compiled by author William Bender Wilson in 1895:

> *The rail line was a significant part of a great North and South line of transportation. [The] PW&B challenged ocean competition and carried on its rails not only statesmen and tourists but a valuable interchange of products between different lines of latitude. As a military highway it was of the greatest strategic importance to the national, industrial, and commercial capitals Washington, Philadelphia, and New York. It presents some of the very best transportation facilities to the commerce of the cities after which it is named, and could not be obliterated from the railroad map of the United States without materially disturbing its harmony.*[1]

The railroad line's significance made it a much-talked-about target for the Confederacy during the start of the Civil War. The Pinkerton Detective Agency had contracted to protect the business from terroristic attacks and to investigate all credible threats to cripple the company.

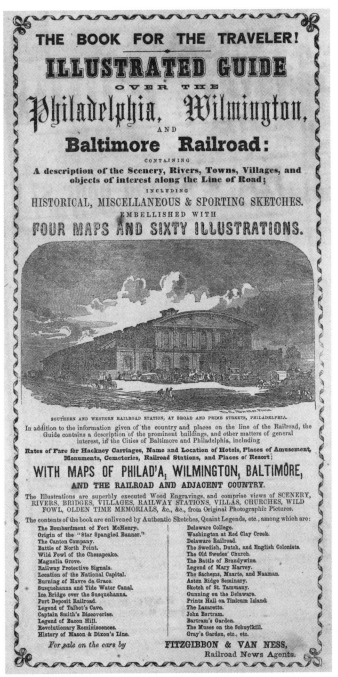

President-elect Abraham Lincoln used the Philadelphia, Wilmington and Baltimore Railroad to travel to Washington, DC, for his inauguration address. COURTESY OF THE LIBRARY OF CONGRESS

It was while Pinkerton was investigating a plan to halt train services in the North that he happened upon a sinister plot that promised to change the political frontier if not stopped.[2]

While posing as the affable John Hutchinson, Pinkerton met a businessman and Southern sympathizer named James H. Luckett. The two men had offices in direct proximity to one another, and in a short time became friends. Luckett was vocal about his desire that Maryland secede from the Union. He was a delegate of a convention of legislature, and he would be presenting his idea to other dedicated secessionists at an upcoming event. Pinkerton pretended to agree with Luckett's political views in hopes that the passionate Rebel would lead the detective to others bent on treason. He did. Luckett introduced Pinkerton to a number of men who belonged to a secret society that had been formed with the goal of creating a slaveholding nation.

In an effort to uncover specific plans the group might have, Pinkerton mentioned the president-elect's trip by train from New York to Washington and what his time in office would mean for the country. "He may pass through Baltimore quietly while en route, but I doubt it," Luckett told Pinkerton, a suspicious grin stretched across his face.[3]

Pinkerton nodded and returned the grin. He understood the inference Luckett made, and why. Daring to continue the topic of conversation, he pointed out that the Baltimore authorities had assured the president-elect's staff safe passage through the city. "Oh, that is easily promised," Luckett stated matter-of-factly, "but may not be so easily done." Although the conspirator showed no restraint in sharing his disdain for Lincoln and the Union, he was not willing to elaborate on what might happen to the politician to interrupt his travels.

Pinkerton reached for his wallet and withdrew $25 in cash, offering it to Luckett. "I've no doubt that money is necessary for the success of this patriotic cause," Pinkerton said. "I would like this donation to be used in the best manner possible for Southern rights." Luckett accepted the money and offered to introduce Pinkerton to the associate who would orchestrate the plan to do away with Mr. Lincoln.[4]

The meeting took place at an eatery on South Street in Baltimore. Captain Cipriano Ferrandini was introduced to Pinkerton as a "true friend of the South." Captain Ferrandini, an Italian revolutionist who tried to kill Napoleon III, was the leader of the group of zealots out to kill the president-elect. The mastermind behind the plan was a barber and a member of the Baltimore militiamen. He organized a number of assassins to shoot Mr. Lincoln as he made his way to the train that would transport him from the city to Washington.[5]

Convinced the plot was more than mere talk, Pinkerton determined he needed to warn Lincoln's security team of the threat. He knew, however, that the president-elect had been bombarded with wild rumors of assassination attempts before, and that it would take a lot to convince Lincoln to take this one seriously.[6]

According to the March 2, 1919, edition of the *San Antonio Light*, Pinkerton's first step was to summon two of his operatives to assist him. One was Kate Warne, and the other, Joseph Howard. Howard was a young man of fine personal appearance and impeccable manners. He was of French descent and careful education. He had lived many years in New Orleans and other Southern cities, and had a thorough knowledge of the South, its localities, prejudices, customs, and leading men. He registered at one of the best Baltimore hotels, giving his home address as New Orleans.[7] The *San Antonio Light* report continued:

> *This proved a passport in the eyes of the "fire eaters" of the city, and Howard was not slow in taking advantage of his opportunity. He noted that business of private capacity required his presence in Baltimore, but as his acquaintances grew more intimate, he admitted that affairs of a national character were far dearer to him than any individual interests or concerns. He soon became a welcomed guest at the most aristocratic homes of the city, and it was not long before he had won the complete confidence of George P. Kane, Chief of Police. From him he learned that the entire police force was in symphony with rebellion, and not only would not protect Lincoln, but would certainly take an active part in any attempt against him.[8]*

Kane invited Howard to a meeting of the secret society, where fiery speeches were delivered, boasting that Lincoln must never be allowed to take over as president. Captain Ferrandini was the leader of the society and incited into a frenzy the crowd that gathered to hear him speak. "This hireling, Lincoln, shall never become president," the captain informed the audience. "My life is of no consequence in a case like this, and I am willing to give it for his. As Orsini gave his life for Italy, I am ready to die for the rights of the South and to crush out abolitionism. In a week from today the North will need another president, for Lincoln will be a corpse."[9]

Joseph Howard managed to find his way into another meeting where the details of when and where Lincoln would be killed and how the assassins were to escape were revealed. With the additional information, Pinkerton hoped Lincoln would take the threat seriously and make the necessary changes to his travel plans. Pinkerton needed the specifics of the plot to convey to the president-elect's head of security, Norman Judd, to convince him to alter their plans. The Lincoln party was making a triumphant trip through the cities of the North and was soon to arrive in New York.[10]

Pinkerton chose Kate Warne as the operative to travel to New York to intercept Lincoln's entourage and deliver to Norman Judd the news Howard had uncovered. Posing as Mrs. M. Barkley, Pinkerton would find Kate sitting in the lobby of a prominent Baltimore hotel, chatting with guests as she worked on a piece of needlework. "Mrs. Warne displayed upon her breast, as did many of the ladies in Baltimore, the black and white cockade, 'which had been temporarily adopted as the emblem of secession,'" Pinkerton noted in the case file. In between special assignments, Kate's job was to gently insinuate herself into conversations between Southern female patrons at various eateries and hotel lobbies.[11]

"She had an ease of manner that was quite captivating," Pinkerton bragged of his protégé. Because Kate was so amiable, she was able to acquire a great deal of information about the location of Confederate troops, subversives, and their plans of attack. "She made remarkable progress in cultivating the acquaintances of wives and daughters of the conspirators," Pinkerton shared years later about Kate. "She was a brilliant conversationalist when so disposed, and could be quite vivacious, but she also understood that rarer quality in womankind, the art of silence."[12]

Kate was surprised to see Allan Pinkerton across the lobby of the hotel where she was working. The protocol was that operatives kept a fair distance from one another so as not to arouse suspicions or risk jeopardizing their cover. The morning of February 7, 1861, Pinkerton was not interested in protocol. He needed to speak to Kate, and when he caught her eye he motioned for her to meet him. Ever so discreetly, she collected her sewing, made excuses to the ladies to whom she had been talking, and headed to her room. Pinkerton followed a safe distance behind, and once inside her private quarters, closed the door behind them.[13]

Quickly and succinctly Pinkerton explained Kate's mission to her. Not only must she deliver the message into Judd's hands, but she also must convince Judd that if Mr. Lincoln passed through Baltimore as planned, his safety could not be guaranteed. She agreed to leave immediately. Pinkerton disappeared from her presence as secretively as he had appeared. Kate wasted no time packing for the trip. She took only the basic essentials, including the message she was to deliver to the president-elect's head of security.[14]

Kate made the trip from Baltimore to New York, continuing to use the alias Mrs. M. Barkley. Letters had been sent ahead of her travels to E. S. Sanford, vice president of the Adams Express Company, and to the president of the American Telegraph Company, with instructions to assist Kate when and if she needed it. The competent operative left Maryland on Monday, February 18, 1861, at 5:16 p.m. She arrived in New York at 4:00 a.m. on Tuesday, February 19, 1861, and checked into the luxury hotel, the Astor House. Arrangements had been made for president-elect Lincoln and his staff to also stay at the hotel. Between six and seven in the morning, Kate left word for Norman Judd to contact her as soon as he arrived. She was exhausted and tried to sleep for a little while, but found she was too anxious to rest. At 7:30 a.m. she adjourned to the dining hall at the establishment for breakfast.[15]

Once Kate finished breakfast, she retired to her room and sat by the window to wait for her party. At roughly three in the afternoon, Mr. Lincoln and his associates arrived via carriage. They were deposited in front of the building. From the hallway outside her room, Kate watched the president-elect's staff file into the lobby. "Lincoln looked very pale and fatigued," Kate noted in her field report. "He was standing in his carriage bowing when I first saw him. From the carriage he went directly into the hotel." A crowd pressed around him as he entered, asking that he deliver an impromptu speech. Kate remembered Lincoln telling the group that he had "nothing to say just now worth your hearing." At the audience's persistence, he offered a few remarks, but according to Kate "there was such a noise it was impossible to hear."[16]

There had been no response from Judd as yet, so Kate sent a second message. At 3:30 p.m. one of Judd's associates contacted the detective and let her know she could send any information she had through him, and he would make sure Judd received it. Kate refused to divulge anything to a second party. She was adamant that only Judd would do, and firmly announced that she would wait to hear from him, but only for a short time.[17]

Norman Judd finally arrived at the Astor House at 7:00 in the evening, when Kate's message was promptly delivered to him. He had missed the Lincoln Special when the train departed ahead of schedule from its last stop. Judd later admitted that he had "never felt so mortified in all his life."[18]

As instructed, he proceeded to Kate's room. The letter the operative handed directly to Lincoln's head of security included a short, initial sentence introducing Kate as the lady superintendent of the Pinkerton Agency. Pinkerton had sent her to New York because he "did not like to trust the mail in so important a matter." Kate informed Judd not to communicate by mail for the same reason. After giving Judd an opportunity to digest the gravity of Pinkerton's note of "importance," Kate offered a brief overview of the situation. "All that needs to be done is to protect Mr. Lincoln," she instructed Judd.[19]

Judd was worried and frustrated. He had numerous questions about Pinkerton's warning, but Kate strongly suggested that he reserve his queries for Pinkerton. Judd didn't seem to find comfort in the idea of waiting. "He said he was much too alarmed and would show the letter I had given him to some of Lincoln's entourage, and also consult with the New York police about it," Kate wrote in her field report. "I told him he was to do no such thing and advised him to keep cool until the meeting with Pinkerton."[20]

Judd lit a cigar and paced the room while Kate continued to reason with him. She briefly contemplated the idea that Pinkerton might have misjudged Judd's ability to keep such a confidence. When the security officer left Kate's room, he was still noncommittal about whether he would stay quiet as Pinkerton directed.

Shortly after Judd excused himself and made his way to his suite, a courier arrived with a telegram for Kate. She immediately requested that Judd return to her room. He was wearing a worried expression when she invited him in and passed the telegram off to him. He quickly opened the message, which read: "Tell Judd I meant all I said, and that today they offer ten for one, and twenty for two." Both Kate and Judd knew what the note meant. Pinkerton was relaying the news from the streets of Baltimore. Sporting men in the city were setting odds that Mr. Lincoln would not pass through the area with his life.[21]

On February 20, 1861, Kate headed back to Baltimore to report to Pinkerton. She was exhausted and preoccupied with the conversation she'd had with Judd the night before. Pinkerton's message not only served to impress upon him the serious threat against Mr. Lincoln's life, but it also instilled a sense of panic. Pinkerton instructed Kate to make arrangements for him to meet Mr. Lincoln in Philadelphia, the next stop on the tour. He wanted to be in the carriage with the president-elect as he rode down the streets of the city, greeting the citizens.[22]

Kate delivered the note to Judd and accompanied the presidential entourage to Philadelphia, where Pinkerton and his advisors met the train. Between the time Kate had returned to New York and Pinkerton boarded the train in Philadelphia, Joseph Howard had uncovered more details about the murder plot. To determine who exactly would deliver the fatal shot, members of Captain Ferrandini's secessionist group placed ballots in a box, declaring that the person who drew a red ballot should perform the assassination. To ensure that no one should know who had drawn the fatal ballot, except the one who did so, the room was made dark, and everyone was pledged to secrecy as to the color of the ballot he drew.

"He [Lincoln] seemed loath to credit the statements and could scarcely believe that such a conspiracy could exist," Pinkerton later wrote about the meeting he had with the president-elect. "Slowly he went over the points presented, questioning me at length, [and] finding it impossible to discredit the truthfulness of what I stated to him, he yielded a reluctant credence to the facts."[23]

"Will you, upon any statement which can be made, consent to leave for Washington on tonight's train?" Judd implored the president-elect.

"No, I can't consent to do this," Mr. Lincoln told him. "I shall hoist the flag on Independence Hall tomorrow morning, and go to Harrisburg tomorrow, and meet the legislature of Pennsylvania; then I shall have fulfilled all my engagements. After this, if you and Mr. Pinkerton think there is still positive danger in my attempting to go through Baltimore openly, according to the published program, if you can arrange any way to carry out your purposes, I will place myself in your hands." Neither Judd nor Pinkerton responded. "Mr. Lincoln had made his position with a tone and manner so decisive," Pinkerton later wrote, "we saw that no more was to be said."[24]

It was finally arranged between Judd, Pinkerton, and the officers of the railroad that a special train should leave Harrisburg at 6:00 p.m. and take Mr. Lincoln to Philadelphia in time to catch the 11:00 p.m. train going through Baltimore to Washington, on the night of February 22. With the help of Kate Warne, this train was to be detained until Mr. Lincoln arrived; every contingency, in regard to the connection of the trains and possible delays, was most skillfully planned, to secure connections and the certainty of going through on time.[25]

Meanwhile, to prevent this change being telegraphed to Baltimore by a Confederate, or information of this change of route being known and getting out in any way, the superintendent of the telegraph company, at the insistence of Mr. Pinkerton, sent a practical telegraph climber to isolate Harrisburg from telegraphic communication with all the world until Mr. Lincoln should reach Washington.[26]

On the morning of February 22, Mr. Lincoln visited Independence Hall and with his own hand raised the flag over it. His speech on this occasion was the most impressive and characteristic of any that he made on his journey to the capital.[27]

"I am filled with deep emotion," president-elect Lincoln told the people who had gathered at Independence Hall, "at finding myself standing in this place where were collected together the wisdom, patriotism, the devotion to principle, from which sprang the institutions which we live. You have kindly suggested to me that in my hands is the task of restoring peace to the present distracted condition of the country. I can say in return, that all the political sentiments I entertain have been drawn, so far as I have been able to draw them, from the sentiments which originated and were given to the world from this hall . . ."[28]

"Liberty as a hope to all the world for all future time was the sentiment which guided those who met here. If this country cannot be saved without giving up that principle, I would rather be assassinated on this spot than surrender it."[29]

The same night Pinkerton disclosed the sinister plan Mr. Lincoln's enemies had conjured, F. W. Seward, Esq., arrived at Philadelphia. He had been sent to Pennsylvania by his father, Secretary of State William Seward, to warn the president-elect of the danger which was awaiting him at Baltimore. Facts had come to the knowledge of Secretary Seward corroborating the evidence which had been accumulated by Mr. Pinkerton of the existence of the conspiracy. This circumstance rendered Mr. Lincoln less reluctant than he had been to consent to the arrangements for his passage through Baltimore on the night of February 22.[30]

From the time the president-elect arrived in Philadelphia, Kate Warne had been working on plans to secret him out of Pennsylvania and into Washington in time for the inauguration. She organized transportation, disguises, and protection. The speech Mr. Lincoln had delivered the day before had created unusual excitement in Baltimore and throughout the South. According to the March 2, 1861, edition of the *Indiana State Guard*, Mr. Lincoln's presentation "embodied sentiments of negro [*sic*] equality which sparked further resentment of the president-elect."[31]

The article continued:

"This indiscreet remark" as Mr. Lincoln himself called it, about lifting the weight from the shoulders of all men, and thus making negros, [sic] as well as whites, free and independent, was really so startling that he seemed to recoil from it, himself, almost before it escaped from his lips, although he declared, a moment or two previously, that he would "rather be assassinated than surrender it."[32]

He was evidently frightened by his own territory, if not by his own shadow, when he reflected that the sentiment of his heart had taken wings, and that the next moment it would reach Baltimore, where it could not fail to excite, to the highest pitch, the population of that slave city. It is to be wondered that he instantly took the cars and hastened off to Harrisburg, shut himself up in his room, and suffered the apprehension of "assassination" to overcome him to such an extent, that he was afraid to receive company after nightfall.[33]

But the idea of "assassination," which took such fearful possession of his mind, was not seriously thought of by anyone else. It was merely the echo of his own words. Secretary Seward, it is true, when he heard of his "indiscreet" speech, and saw its effect, politically, upon the country, concluded that the sooner he took him in charge, the better for the interests of the incoming administration. But the idea of "assassination" if it entered the mind of the Premier, was only in the shape of another "good enough, Morgan," which would answer his purpose until after the inauguration, or, at all events, until he had secured the seals of the State Department.[34]

The tension surrounding the president-elect taking office was palpable. The *Indiana State Guard* article echoed the sentiments many Southern sympathizers embraced.

At 3:00 a.m. on February 23, 1861, Pinkerton met Kate in her room to go over the final details of the plan to get Lincoln out of the city without anyone knowing. The report Kate wrote regarding the particulars of the plan noted that Pinkerton appeared "sick and tired out." Prior to the serious threats made on his life, Mr. Lincoln and his staff were to travel from Philadelphia to Harrisburg, then to Baltimore via the Northern Central Railroad. Only a handful of people were aware that slight alterations had been made to the schedule and passenger list. The Northern Central train Mr. Lincoln was initially set to board, transporting him to Baltimore and on to Washington, would leave as planned. Those awaiting the president-elect's arrival had no idea he wouldn't be on the vehicle. Mr. Lincoln would make the anticipated stop in Harrisburg and then secretly change trains there. The Northern Central would continue on as though Mr. Lincoln were on board.[35]

Mr. Lincoln's itinerary in Harrisburg was filled with meetings, speeches, and meals with supporters and politicians. His evening ended at 5:45 p.m. on February 23, after dining with the governor of Pennsylvania. Mr. Lincoln retired to his room, ostensibly to go to bed early because he was exhausted. What he did instead was change his clothing in preparation to leave the city. When he was ushered out the back door of the house, he was wearing an old overcoat and carrying a soft, wool hat. He had left behind his usual beaver, stovepipe hat and walked outside bareheaded, unrecognized by strangers.[36]

President-elect Lincoln was committed to following through with the Pinkerton Detective Agency's plan, but questioned the opinion his constituents would have regarding his actions. "What would the nation think of its president stealing into the capital like a thief in the night?" Pennsylvania senator Alexander K. McClure later recalled Mr. Lincoln sharing with him.[37]

Dressed in black taffeta, Kate Warne waited in the shadows of the Philadelphia, Wilmington and Baltimore Railroad depot for Mr. Lincoln. She was confident she and the other Pinkerton operatives on the case had done all that was necessary to ensure the president-elect's safety, but in the dark, contemplating all that could happen, it seemed the whole world was against Lincoln. An article in the February 22, 1861, edition of the *Warren Mail* reported that the public was being unfair to the incoming president, and that such harsh criticism of him could "bring down the government and destroy the future of the country."[38] The article continued:

Never since the days of Washington has a candidate been less the object of personal crimination and slander than Abraham Lincoln! So

perfectly faultless has been his private life and character that his ene-
mies could not truly discover the semblance of a flow upon which they
might seize, and distort into something out of which to manufacture
their political capitol.[39]

If then there is nothing in the man or the principles he represents
to justify the spirit of revolution which pervades the entire South,
what is the real cause of the discontent . . . ?[40]

A portion of the States have revolted and are now in open rebel-
lion against the Federal authorities. . . .[41]

Mr. Lincoln is now on his way to the Capital. He will call to his
aid the best talent the country can produce. The rights of all sections
of the country will be respected and enforced, as well as those of the
general government.[42]

To those who oppose the shedding of blood to perpetuate the
Union, we would say, our fathers obtained the liberty we enjoy at
the expense of the seven-year war; and by the grace of God we will
continue to defend and protect it, peacefully if we can, forcibly if we
must . . .[43]

We trust the spirit of patriotism which enabled the founders of our
Republic to safely launch the Ship of State will also enable incoming
administrations to preserve intact her massive timbers in the storm
through which she is now passing, and to see the new leader safely to
office.[44]

Kate Warne and the other members of the Pinkerton Detective
Agency on assignment to watch over Mr. Lincoln would go to great
lengths to make sure the new leader was delivered safely to office. Until
the time Mr. Lincoln took the oath of office, Kate would be on guard for
anyone who suspected the president-elect had deviated from the original
touring schedule. Pinkerton had warned all of his operatives to remember
that the rebellion was just as dedicated to doing away with Mr. Lincoln
as they were to keeping him from harm.[45]

Pinkerton required his operatives to memorize the letter he had
received from the master mechanic of the PW&B Railroad about the
plans to take the president-elect's life. "I am informed that a son of a

distinguished citizen of Maryland said he had taken an oath with others to assassinate Mr. Lincoln before he gets to Washington," the railroad contact's letter read. "They may attempt to do it while he is passing over our road. Take every precaution."

It would take courage and skill to save the life of Mr. Lincoln and prevent the revolution that would inevitably follow his violent death. Like Pinkerton, Kate believed it could be accomplished, and she wouldn't allow herself a moment's peace until the job was done.[46]

NOTES

1. Wilson, *History of the Pennsylvania Railroad Department of the Young Men's Christian Association of Pennsylvania*, pp. 14–17.
2. Ibid.
3. Recko, *A Spy for the Union*, pp. 51–54.
4. Ibid.
5. Horan, *The Pinkertons*, pp. 55–57.
6. Ibid.
7. *San Antonio Light*, March 2, 1919.
8. Ibid.
9. Ibid.
10. Moran, *The Eye That Never Sleeps*, pp. 39–41; Horan, *The Pinkertons*, pp. 57–58.
11. Stashower, *The Hour of Peril*, p. 195.
12. Ibid., pp. 104, 195–96.
13. Horan, *The Pinkertons*, pp. 53–59.
14. Horan, *The Pinkertons*, pp. 53–59; *San Antonio Light*, March 2, 1919.
15. Horan, *The Pinkertons*, pp. 53–59; Stashower, *The Hour of Peril*, pp. 142–43, 204–08.
16. Horan, *The Pinkertons*, pp. 53–59.
17. Stashower, *The Hour of Peril*, pp. 204–08.
18. Ibid.
19. Stashower, *The Hour of Peril*, pp. 204–08; Moran, *The Eye That Never Sleeps*, pp. 39–41.
20. Stashower, *The Hour of Peril*, pp. 204–08; Horan, *The Pinkertons*, pp. 53–59.
21. Stashower, *The Hour of Peril*, pp. 204–08.
22. Stashower, *The Hour of Peril*, pp. 204–08; Horan, *The Pinkertons*, pp. 53–59.
23. *Harper's Magazine*, June 1868.
24. Ibid.
25. *Harper's Magazine*, June 1868; Stashower, *The Hour of Peril*, pp. 250–53; Horan, *The Pinkertons*, pp. 53–59.
26. *Harper's Magazine*, June 1868; Stashower, *The Hour of Peril*, pp. 247–48.
27. Stashower, *The Hour of Peril*, pp. 247–48.
28. National Archives, Lincoln's Address in Independence Hall, February 1861.
29. Ibid.

30. Stashower, *The Hour of Peril*, pp. 239–40.

31. *Indiana State Guard*, March 2, 1861.

32. Ibid.

33. Ibid.

34. Ibid.

35. Stashower, *The Hour of Peril*, pp. 245–47.

36. Stashower, *The Hour of Peril*, pp. 245–47; Horan, *The Pinkertons*, 53–59.

37. Horan, *The Pinkertons*, 53–59.

38. Stashower, *The Hour of Peril*, pp. 245–47; Horan, *The Pinkertons*, 53–59; *Warren Mail*, February 22, 1861.

39. *Warren Mail*, February 22, 1861.

40. Ibid.

41. Ibid.

42. Ibid.

43. Ibid.

44. Ibid.

45. Pinkerton, *Spy of the Rebellion*, pp. 54–57.

46. Pinkerton, *Spy of the Rebellion*, pp. 54–57; Horan, *The Pinkertons*, pp. 53–59.

CHAPTER FIVE

OPERATIVE BARKLEY IN WASHINGTON

PRESIDENT-ELECT ABRAHAM LINCOLN SHOWED NO SIGN OF BEING NERvous or apprehensive about the late-night ride Pinkerton operatives arranged for him to take on February 23, 1861. Kate Warne noted in her records of the events surrounding Mr. Lincoln leaving Pennsylvania that he was cooperative and congenial.[1]

When the politician arrived at the depot in Baltimore with his colleagues and confidants, Ward Hill Lamon and Allan Pinkerton, he was focused and quiet. He was stooped over and leaning on Pinkerton's arm. The posture helped to disguise his height, and when Kate greeted him with a slight hug and called him "Brother," no one outside the small group thought anything of the exchange. For all anyone knew, Kate and Mr. Lincoln were siblings embarking on a trip together. Neither the porter nor the train's brakeman recognized Mr. Lincoln as the president-elect. Kate made it clear to the limited railroad staff on board that her brother was not well and in need of solitude.[2]

It took a mere two minutes from the time the distinguished orator reached the depot until he and his companions were comfortably on board the special train. The conductor was instructed to leave the station only after he was handed a package Pinkerton had told him to expect. The conductor was informed that the package contained important government documents that needed to be kept secret and delivered to

Washington with "great haste." In truth the documents were a bundle of newspapers wrapped and sealed.[3]

The bell on the engine clanged, and the train lurched forward. The gas lamps in the sleeping berths in Mr. Lincoln's car were not lit, and the shades were pulled. Kate and Pinkerton agreed it would be best to prevent curious passengers waiting at various stops from seeing in and possibly identifying the president-elect. No one spoke as the train slowly pulled away from the station. All hoped the journey would be uneventful, and were hesitant to make a sound for fear any conversation might jeopardize what had been done to get Mr. Lincoln to this point. It was Mr. Lincoln who broke the silence with an amusing story he had shared with Pennsylvania governor Andrew Curtain the previous evening.[4]

"I used to know an old farmer out in Illinois," Mr. Lincoln told the three around him. "He took it into his head to venture into raising hogs. So he sent out to Europe and imported the finest breed of hogs that he could buy. The prize hog was put in a pen and the farmer's two mischievous boys, James and John, were told to be sure not to let it out. But James let the brute out the very next day. The hog went straight for the boys and drove John up a tree. Then it went for the seat of James's trousers, and the only way the boy could save himself was by holding on to the porker's tail. The hog would not give up his hunt or the boy his hold. After they had made a good many circles around the tree, the boy's courage began to give out, and he shouted to his brother: " 'I say, John, come down quick and help me let go of this hog.' "[5]

Mr. Lincoln's traveling companions smiled politely and stifled a chuckle. Had the circumstances been different, perhaps they would have laughed aloud. Undaunted by the trio's subdued response, the president-elect continued to regale them with amusing tales of the people he'd met and experiences they'd shared. The train gained speed, and soon Philadelphia was disappearing behind them.[6]

After a while, Kate and her fellow passengers retired to their sleeping berths. As she closed the drapes hanging in front of the president-elect's berth, she suggested he stay out of sight until they reached their destination. In Kate's report she noted that Mr. Lincoln was "so very tall that he could not lay straight in his berth." She proceeded to the bunk where Pinkerton was tucked inside and presented to him the reports George

Dunn had compiled about the assassination plot. Pinkerton had barely had a chance to review the material when the conductor, making his rounds, approached, requesting tickets. Kate, wearing a tearful expression, intercepted the conductor. She quickly handed her and Mr. Lincoln's tickets to him. "My brother is a sick man," she explained to the conductor, "and has already retired." The conductor nodded sympathetically and took the tickets from her. Pinkerton surrendered his ticket and Ward Hill Lamon's ticket at the same time. The conductor carried on without question.[7]

Lamon checked his watch as Kate and Pinkerton climbed into their individual berths. Not only was he anxious about what might happen during the four-and-a-half-hour journey to Washington, but he was also frustrated with Pinkerton. Prior to boarding the train, Lamon had offered his bowie knife to Mr. Lincoln to carry with him, in case he was attacked. Pinkerton objected to the idea. "I would not for the world have it said that Mr. Lincoln had to enter the capital armed," Pinkerton wrote in his report about the exchange. "If fighting has to be done, it must be done by others than Mr. Lincoln."[8]

None of the four slept. The president-elect talked softly to his tense, fellow passengers from behind the closed curtain of his berth. "He talked very friendly for some time," Kate recalled in her notes about the trip. "The excitement seemed to keep us all awake."[9]

The most worrisome part of the journey was yet to come. All the members of the party were preoccupied thinking of it. Pinkerton couldn't stay still. He would alternate between sitting for a few moments, lying back in his berth, pacing, and walking to the rear door of the car to keep watch from the back platform. Pinkerton arranged for his operatives to leave a series of signals along the route should assassins plot to destroy the tracks and derail the train. Pinkerton had watchmen placed at various intervals along the track. They waved lanterns to show that the coast was clear.[10]

As the train approached Perrymansville, a critical point of the trip, it slowed to a crawl as it neared the Susquehanna River. Here, the cars of the train had to be uncoupled and ferried across the water. Pinkerton feared that if Mr. Lincoln had been spotted leaving Pennsylvania and assassins had tracked him to the slowing train, it would provide a perfect opportunity to kill him. Rebels could set the ferry on fire, and any attempt to rescue the president-elect from the blaze and get him to shore could be met with gunfire.[11]

Just before Lincoln's car was set to be shuttled across the river, Kate crawled out of her berth and sat in a chair next to Mr. Lincoln's berth. She did not move from his side for the duration of the trip. According to Kate's report,

> *There was no doubt Mr. Lincoln was uneasy about this part of the trip. The echo of his own words at Independence Hall, Philadelphia, when he declared he would "rather be assassinated on the spot" than abandon his ideas of independence and equality for all, rang in his head. His spirits were bolstered by the fact that Pinkerton had "taken every precaution to protect him from insult and annoyance, and to do honor to him as the president-elect, if not to the man.[12]*

In addition to the possibility of the ferry being attacked was the danger inherent with transporting railcars across the river by boat. Train carriages were difficult to secure; they had to be tightly strapped lest they break away and roll around. A significant amount of water could destabilize the ferry and cause the carriages to tip. The entire process of loading the railcars onto the ferry, sending them across the river, unloading the railcars, and coupling them together again took more than forty minutes. When the last car was placed back on the track and the train's engine was once again started, Pinkerton and Kate breathed a collective sigh of relief. "We are getting along very well," Pinkerton reported Mr. Lincoln as saying. "I think we are on time," he added. "I cannot realize how any man situated as he was could have shown more calmness or firmness," Pinkerton recalled of the president-elect.[13]

Without mishap the train pressed on, running through the very stronghold of Lincoln's angriest border opponents. The train reached Baltimore at 3:30 in the morning. Kate peered out at a city she knew would be aboil with plots of disunion.[14]

Like all pioneer railroads, the Philadelphia, Wilmington and Baltimore cars bound for the capital had to be drawn through the city thoroughfares by horses to the station of the Washington line. The party moved surreptitiously through the streets to meet the train that would take Mr. Lincoln into Washington.[15]

Despite the late hour, numerous people had congregated in that quarter of the city and were singing and celebrating. The connecting train Mr. Lincoln's entourage was to meet was late, and several tense moments passed before news of its impending arrival was made known to Pinkerton. Once or twice Kate felt the partisan revelers milling dangerously close. "Perhaps at this moment the reckless conspirators were astir perfecting their plans for a tragedy as infamous as any which has ever disgraced a free country," Pinkerton wrote about that stressful time the quartet spent contemplating their fate on the way to the next depot. "Perhaps even now the holders of the red ballots were nerving themselves for their part in the dreadful work, or were tossing restlessly upon sleepless couches."[16]

Kate, Pinkerton, Lamon, and Mr. Lincoln would have to wait two hours for the connecting train to pull into the depot. All the while, the president-elect remained in his berth, joking with those around him. Occasionally, when all was silent inside the car, choruses of the songs "My Maryland" and "Dixie" could be heard coming from the waiting passengers. After one obviously intoxicated individual belted out the last stanza of "Dixie," Mr. Lincoln peered out the curtains of his berth and smiled. "No doubt there will be a great time in Dixie by and by," he told his protectors.[17]

At 5:35 in the morning, two Pinkerton operatives who were also employed to keep the Philadelphia, Wilmington and Baltimore line safe and secure entered the rear of the compartment. Pinkerton greeted the men, and one of them announced to the detective that "All was right." Pinkerton thanked the men for their diligence and escorted them out of the car. Kate followed along behind them. While Pinkerton was giving the two operatives instructions for the final leg of the journey, Kate strode off into the night. Her job was done. She'd provided the necessary cover Mr. Lincoln required to get him to Baltimore, and in a short time he would be at the nation's capital. It would not have been looked upon favorably to have the president-elect arrive with a woman who was not his wife. Even if that woman was a detective, the uninformed would talk.[18]

Kate heard the car carrying Mr. Lincoln being coupled to the train that would transport him to Washington. Pinkerton climbed back on board, and the train whistle blew. Kate paused a moment to listen to the engine firing and beginning to pull its load away from the depot. Once the train was on its way, she hailed a carriage to take her into the city where the next job she was to handle would be awaiting her.[19]

Nothing occurred to delay or interrupt the remainder of the president-elect's trip. Pinkerton, Lamon, and Mr. Lincoln arrived in Washington at 6:00 in the morning of February 23. Mr. Lincoln exited the car wrapped in his traveling shawl. A great many people had gathered at the depot, but Mr. Lincoln made it through the crowd without anyone recognizing him. Just as the president-elect was about to leave the depot area, Elihu B. Washburne—a member of Lincoln's security detail, and one of the men who personally severed the telegraph wires to keep information from being transferred back and forth from Baltimore and Washington—extended his arm and attempted to shake the president-elect's hand. "How are you, Mr. Lincoln?" Washburne asked. Pinkerton was taken aback by Washburne's boldness, and fearing Mr. Lincoln's cover might be compromised, punched Washburne in the face before he could utter another word. Lincoln broke in and stopped Pinkerton from striking the man again. The detective quickly realized his error, and the overreaction was attributed to the stressful circumstances surrounding the efforts to get the president-elect safely to the capital.[20]

Within twenty-four hours of arriving in Washington, Mr. Lincoln asked the detectives that had played a part in making sure he was delivered unharmed to meet him at the home where he was staying, situated across from the White House. Kate was absent from the gathering, but the president-elect made sure to list "his sister" as one of the many to thank for her help.[21]

On the afternoon of February 24, 1861, Kate Warne as Mrs. Barkley met with fellow operative Harry Davies at Barnum's Hotel in Baltimore. News that Mr. Lincoln had passed through the city unnoticed and unannounced had created quite a stir among citizens. Some residents were

Crowd at the first inauguration of President Abraham Lincoln COURTESY OF THE
LIBRARY OF CONGRESS

disappointed that they'd missed seeing the president-elect on his inaugural trip, and others were insulted that he chose to bypass their town. Kate, Davies, and other Pinkerton detectives in Baltimore had encountered angry citizens who believed they had been slighted intentionally by the government. The detectives anticipated those who had plotted against Mr. Lincoln would band together to mull over their thwarted assassination plan. Pinkerton had asked his agents to gather any information about renewed efforts to kill Mr. Lincoln.[22]

The February 25, 1861, edition of the *New York Times* reported the mood in Baltimore and tried to explain to readers why Mr. Lincoln decided not to stop over in the city:

> *Mr. Lincoln's coup d'état and rapid passage through the city have been condemned here by some who do not know the facts. A set of unscrupulous political knaves . . . who had determined to turn Mr. Lincoln's visit there to their own account, arranged for a procession from the depot to his hotel. Protection was asked by these rowdies of Marshal Kane [Baltimore's police marshal], who advised against such a proceeding. He said Mr. Lincoln would be treated with all respect due him personally and his high official position, but so obnoxious were the parties proposing the demonstration that he could not ensure the same respect to them. If they were determined to brave the matter, it might result in some indignity being offered which would be mortifying to the President-elect and disgraceful to the City of Baltimore.[23]*
>
> *Finding that these men were fixed in their purposes, the latter was advised by telegraph to pass on to Washington without stopping, which he did. This advice came from gentlemen who had the good name of Baltimore chiefly at heart.[24]*
>
> *These advices [sic] from Baltimore had been anticipated by a special messenger sent hence to meet Mr. Lincoln at Philadelphia, with dispatches from the War Department, urging him to come through Baltimore unexpectedly, as they had specific information of hostile purposes against him there, in relation to which they could not be mistaken. This information was obtained through official secret agents.[25]*

Pinkerton was furious after reading the articles that announced the facts about the plot against Mr. Lincoln had been acquired by secret agents. All players involved in the plans to get the president-elect to the capital safely were sworn to keep quiet about all matters relating to Lincoln's trip to Washington. Pinkerton suspected Elihu B. Washburne had spoken to the press in retaliation for punching him. Pinkerton believed the leaked information would compromise his agents in Baltimore. He wanted to make sure Kate and the other operatives were more careful than they had been about getting caught spying. Until the would-be assassins were discovered and arrested, Pinkerton agents were at risk. Pinkerton returned to the city as quickly as he could to resume the undercover work he was doing prior to escorting the president-elect to the capital.[26]

From late February to early April 1861, Kate spent the bulk of her time in the parlor of Barnum's Hotel. Many of the wives of Southern businessmen, lawyers, and politicians staying at the establishment congregated in an open room connected to the lobby. The women would share news of the unrest between the states and pass along tidbits their husbands told them, or that they overheard. Kate would pass along to Lincoln any information that would advance the cause of the Union. Operative Hattie Lawton was doing the same at the hotel where she resided as well. The two women and other female detectives working for Pinkerton were positioned throughout the town in libraries, eateries, and stage and train depots, all in hopes of hearing news worthy of being passed along. Pinkerton believed war was inevitable, but wasn't sure what position Maryland would take. A large and influential minority of people in the state were in favor of secession. Pinkerton wanted to know who would conspire against the Union.[27]

On April 12, 1861, the first engagement between the United States and the Confederate States began. Fort Sumter was attacked by Confederate troops, and President Lincoln recommended war, calling for an army of 75,000. Not long after the fort in South Carolina was overtaken, Pinkerton decided that his agency had to be at the president's service. Operative Timothy Webster was selected as the agent to transport more than a dozen dispatches to Washington. Kate Warne concealed those messages by sewing them into the lining and collar of Webster's waistcoat.[28] One of Pinkerton's letters began,

Dear Sir,
When I saw you last I said that if the time should ever come that I could be of service to you, I was ready. If that time has come, I am on hand.[29]

I have in my force from sixteen to eighteen persons on whose courage, skill, and devotion to their country I can rely. If they, with myself at the head, can be of service in the way of obtaining information of the movements of the traitors, or safely conveying your letters or dispatches, or that class of Secret Service which is the most dangerous, I am at your command.[30]

In the present disturbed state of affairs I dare not trust this to the mail, so send by one of my force who was with me at Baltimore. You may safely trust him with any message for me, written or verbal. I fully guarantee his fidelity. He will act as you direct and return here with your answer.[31]

Secrecy is the great lever I propose to operate with, hence the necessity of this movement (if you contemplate it) being kept strictly private, and that should you desire another interview with the Bearer, that you should so arrange it that he will not be noticed. The Bearer will hand you a copy of a telegraphic cipher which you may use if you desire to telegram me.[32]

My forces comprise both sexes, all of good character and well skilled in their business.

Respectfully yours,
Allan Pinkerton[33]

In May of 1861, President Lincoln ordered the formation of a military secret service. Major General George McClellan was named the head of the organization; Allan Pinkerton was in command, directly under the general. Both McClellan and Lincoln agreed that Pinkerton and his operatives could be trusted to uncover traitors and carry secret dispatches. Pinkerton moved his operation to Washington, along with key personnel. Kate was promoted to the head of the female division of the Secret Service. Her job, as well as that of the other agents, was to investigate suspicious people within the Union territory and gather information from behind Confederate lines. Both endeavors required the strictest secrecy. Kate and the other operatives were supplied with a variety of disguises and equipped with a theatrical wardrobe.[34]

Allan Pinkerton, chief of McClellan's Secret Service, with his men near Cumberland Landing, Virginia COURTESY OF THE NATIONAL ARCHIVES, PHOTO NO. 522914

The Pinkerton National Detective Agency had a number of offices, one each in Washington, Baltimore, Chicago, and Cincinnati. Kate was assigned the Ohio office, not far from McClellan's division. Posing as a Southern belle, she traveled to Virginia and Tennessee, frequenting social events with genuine Southern ladies who were married or engaged to Rebel soldiers. These belles would often share details their significant others told them about where and when the Confederate Army was moving. Such information was passed along to McClellan and Pinkerton.[35]

Later during the month of May, Kate and a handful of other operatives were meeting with Pinkerton at his Washington office on I Street when a prominent leader in the capital told them about a woman who was suspected of being a Confederate spy.[36]

According to Pinkerton's memoirs, the lady was Rose Greenhow, a Southern woman of "pronounced Rebel proclivities, and who had been unsparing in her denunciation of the 'Abolition North,' and who had openly declared that instead of loving and worshipping the old flag of the Stars and Stripes, she saw in it only the symbol of murder, plunder, oppression, and shame." Pinkerton planned to utilize all the agents in his employ to combat the influential spy. Kate's assignment in the battle was key, and evolved as the investigation played out.[37]

Now a widow, Rose Greenhow had been born in 1814 on a farm in Montgomery County, Maryland. When she was thirteen, she was sent to live with her aunt and uncle in Washington. Her relatives were close, with a number of people who were advocates of slavery and states' rights. As she grew older, she adopted their viewpoint and became not only a supporter of the Confederate cause, but also a spokesperson for the rebellion. At the age of twenty-one, she met and married Washington's most eligible and well-respected bachelor, Dr. Robert Greenhow. Her new husband's position, combined with her beauty, refined manners, and congenial personality, catapulted her to the top of the social scene. Rose was as cunning and smart as she was attractive, and focused on cultivating friendships with the leading figures in the city.[38]

She was well acquainted with James Buchanan, northern Democrats, and Southern sympathizers. In 1856 she had encouraged Buchanan to run for the presidency, and helped to raise funds and voters needed for him to receive the nomination. Rose was good friends with political leaders such as senators William H. Seward of New York, Henry Wilson of Massachusetts, and Stephen A. Douglas of Illinois. Her association with army leaders, politicians, and the affluent earned her a reputation as the woman ambitious legislators needed to know to get anything accomplished in government.[39]

When Abraham Lincoln was elected to office in 1860, Rose's influence dwindled to nothing. Furious that a Republican and antislavery activist was now in the White House, she decided to rail against the system. Seven states seceded from the Union, and the majority of the Southern supporters left the capital. Rose refused to relocate and vowed to stay and fight for the cause.[40]

Simon Cameron, the secretary of war, ordered Pinkerton to carefully watch Rose Greenhow's home and monitor the people who visited. In the summer of 1861, it was discovered that Rose had been recruited by a Confederate spy ring to join their ranks. Her job was to secure military secrets. Pinkerton tasked three agents with surveillance and ordered them to follow anyone who might seem questionable. Kate was one of the operatives assigned to keep tabs on those individuals coming and going from Rose's home.[41]

Rose did not work alone. She solicited help from a handful of women in the area capable of charming necessary information from weak-minded men. In the short time Rose and her agents had been collecting secrets, they had acquired letters from the War and Engineering Departments. Correspondence from both departments included descriptions of the government's troop numbers, maps, and locations. "I desired to obtain a thorough insight into all the plans and schemes of these who were to become the prominent actors in the fearful drama [Civil War]," Rose wrote in her memoirs years after the South lost to the North, "in order that I might turn it to the advantage of my country when the hour of action arrived."[42]

In July 1861, one of Rose's girls came across a message from a Union soldier containing information about placement near the city of Manassas not far from the capital city. Using the cover name of Thomas John Rayford, Rose sent a message via courier to Confederate general P. G. T. Beauregard. The message informed the Rebel officer that 55,000 Union troops were going to march out of Arlington Heights and Alexandria and on to Manassas. A chain of couriers was used to relay messages from the battlefield to Rose and back again. Men and women who worked on the chain were positioned along secret routes that connected Washington and Baltimore to the Confederacy. Rose sometimes used her eight-year-old daughter to deliver messages.[43]

Pinkerton considered it unfortunate that Rose and her cohorts weren't discovered before the Battle at Bull Run. The numerous messages she managed to secret to the Confederate generals led to the downfall of the Union Army on that occasion. General Beauregard was able to reinforce the battle lines with 12,000 more soldiers than the North had anticipated. Southern president Jefferson Davis sent word of his thanks, and added in his dispatch, "We rely upon you for further information. The Confederacy owes you a debt."[44]

Kate Warne and the two other operatives Pinkerton had assigned to keep tabs on Rose began their job in earnest in late July 1861. Pinkerton joined their efforts. Rose entertained a myriad of guests from July 23 through August 22. She was a celebrity of sorts, and intelligence gathered by Pinkerton and his agents attributed her rise in popularity to the Secret Service work she had done for the Confederacy. She was not shy about expressing her dislike for President Lincoln and his wife. Her open criticism of the administration and the insulting remarks made about the First Lady sparked more than a passing interest from loyal Northerners.[45]

While Kate spent time attending various social engagements where Rose was present, Pinkerton and two other agents investigated the Rebel spy's two-story house. On August 20, 1861, the detectives gathered at the Greenhow home to find out what they could about who came and went. The weather that day was dark, gloomy, and threatening. Pinkerton was lifted to the upstairs windows to look inside. While he was snooping around, Rose and a soldier arrived. She welcomed the soldier inside and escorted him into the parlor. Pinkerton recognized the man as a Union captain of infantry in charge of one of the stations of the provost marshal. He watched the pair sitting across from one another and talking. Pinkerton heard enough to convince him that the trusted officer was engaged in betraying his country. "He was furnishing his treasonable companion with information regarding the disposition of our troops as he possessed," Pinkerton later wrote in his report to the secretary of war.[46]

"He took from an inner pocket of his coat a map which, as he held it up before the light, I imagined that I could identify as a plan of the fortifications in and around Washington; and which also designated a contemplated plan of attack.[47]

"After watching their movements for some time, during which they would frequently refer to the map before them, as though pointing out particular points or positions, I was compelled to rush into the room."[48]

Pinkerton controlled himself, however, and waited until the captain had left Rose's home at 12:15 a.m. He quietly followed the captain as he strolled down Pennsylvania Avenue. At some point the officer sensed someone was behind him and quickened his pace; Pinkerton did the same. The pursuit ended at the captain's barracks when four armed soldiers interrupted the chase, apprehended the detective, and threw him in jail.[49]

Kate, Pryce Lewis, and Sam Bridgeman were left behind at Rose's house, unaware of the trouble Pinkerton had encountered. No one knew about Pinkerton's imprisonment until the resourceful detective bribed a guard to notify Thomas Scott, assistant secretary of war, of his situation. Scott had Pinkerton transferred to the War Department for a personal interrogation, and during the questioning Pinkerton revealed what he had discovered. Scott ordered the captain to be brought before him. The officer denied he'd been anywhere near Rose Greenhow's residence, but he wasn't convincing. Scott told him to surrender, and he was subsequently arrested. Incriminating papers were found among his effects, and he was imprisoned in Fort McHenry. There is evidence that the traitor might have been Captain John Ellwood, who fell into further trouble and later killed himself by cutting his throat with a penknife.[50]

Neither Rose Greenhow nor Allan Pinkerton identified Ellwood in their memoirs, but the Pennsylvania Archives of Civil War Soldiers notes that he was the miscreant Pinkerton saw with Rose. Pinkerton's report to Scott, provided to him by Kate, contained the names of several prominent gentlemen in Washington who visited Rose.[51]

Assistant Secretary Scott declared that Mrs. Greenhow was a dangerous character who must at least be attended to "and issued an order for her arrest."[52]

Kate Warne watched in the near distance as her fellow operatives, accompanied by Union soldiers, congregated at the Greenhow home and made their way inside. Kate was prepared to do whatever was asked of her to destroy the spy ring that had altered the course of the early days of the Civil War.

NOTES

1. Horan, *The Pinkertons*, pp. 53–61; *Richmond Dispatch*, February 23, 1861; Stashower, *The Hour of Peril*, pp. 272–78.
2. Pinkerton, *History and Evidence of the Passage of Abraham Lincoln from Harrisburg to Washington*, pp. 17, 28, 35; Cuthbert, *Lincoln and the Baltimore Plot*, pp. 52–58.
3. Pinkerton, *History and Evidence*, pp. 17, 28, 35.
4. Stashower, *The Hour of Peril*, p. 279; Pinkerton, *History and Evidence*, pp. 17, 28, 35; Cuthbert, *Lincoln and the Baltimore Plot*, pp. 52–58.
5. *Richmond Dispatch*, February 23, 1861; *Newbern Weekly Progress*, February 26, 1861.
6. *Newbern Weekly Progress*, February 26, 1861.

7. Pinkerton, *History and Evidence*, pp. 17, 28, 35; Cuthbert, *Lincoln and the Baltimore Plot*, pp. 52–58.

8. Horan, *The Pinkertons*, pp. 53–61; Stashower, *The Hour of Peril*, pp. 277–78.

9. Horan, *The Pinkertons*, pp. 53–61.

10. Pinkerton, *History and Evidence*, pp. 17, 28, 35; Cuthbert, *Lincoln and the Baltimore Plot*, pp. 52–58.

11. Cuthbert, *Lincoln and the Baltimore Plot*, pp. 52–58.

12. Horan, *The Pinkertons*, pp. 53–61; *Indiana State Guard*, March 2, 1861.

13. *Indiana State Guard*, March 2, 1861.

14. Horan, *The Pinkertons*, pp. 53–61; *Indiana State Guard*, March 2, 1861; *The American Weekly Magazine*, February 11, 1951.

15. Pinkerton, *Spy of the Rebellion*, pp. 95–97.

16. Ibid., pp. 98–108.

17. Ibid.

18. Stashower, *The Hour of Peril*, pp. 281–85.

19. Ibid.

20. Stashower, *The Hour of Peril*, pp. 281–85; Pinkerton, *History and Evidence*, pp. 17, 28, 35; Cuthbert, *Lincoln and the Baltimore Plot*, pp. 52–58.

21. Stashower, *The Hour of Peril*, pp. 287–88.

22. Pinkerton, *History and Evidence*, pp. 17, 28, 35; Cuthbert, *Lincoln and the Baltimore Plot*, pp. 52–58.

23. *New York Times*, February 25, 1861.

24. Ibid.

25. Ibid.

26. Stashower, *The Hour of Peril*, pp. 295–96; Pinkerton, *History and Evidence*, pp. 17, 28, 35; Cuthbert, *Lincoln and the Baltimore Plot*, pp. 52–58; *Fayetteville Weekly Observer*, March 4, 1861; *Janesville Weekly Gazette*, March 8, 1861.

27. Pinkerton, *Spy of the Rebellion*, pp. 108–11.

28. *Memphis Daily Appeal*, April 13, 1861.

29. *Memphis Daily Appeal*, April 13, 1861; National Archives, Intelligence in the Civil War.

30. *Memphis Daily Appeal*, April 13, 1861; National Archives, Intelligence in the Civil War; Pinkerton, *Spy of the Rebellion*, pp. 108–11; *The National Tribune*, November 8, 1900.

31. *Memphis Daily Appeal*, April 13, 1861; National Archives, Intelligence in the Civil War; Pinkerton, *Spy of the Rebellion*, pp. 108–11; *The National Tribune*, November 8, 1900.

32. *Memphis Daily Appeal*, April 13, 1861; National Archives, Intelligence in the Civil War; Pinkerton, *Spy of the Rebellion*, pp. 108–11.

33. *Memphis Daily Appeal*, April 13, 1861; National Archives, Intelligence in the Civil War; Pinkerton, *Spy of the Rebellion*, pp. 108–11; *The National Tribune*, November 8, 1900; *Memphis Daily Appeal*, April 13, 1861.

34. Library of Congress, McClellan Papers, July 22, 1861, July 25, 1861; Moran, *The Eye That Never Sleeps*, p. 43; *St. Johnsbury Caledonian*, July 17, 1884.

35. Horan, *The Pinkertons*, pp. 62–77.
36. Ibid.
37. Ibid.
38. Winkler, *Stealing Secrets*, pp. 3–5.
39. Winkler, *Stealing Secrets*, pp. 3–5; *Syracuse Herald*, October 7, 1911; *Boston Sunday Post*, October 31, 1915.
40. Pinkerton, *Spy of the Rebellion*, pp. 254–59. Winkler, *Stealing Secrets*, pp. 14–21.
41. Ibid.
42. Ross, *Rebel Rose: The Life of Rose O'Neal Greenhow*, pp. 100–03.
43. Ibid.
44. Ross, *Rebel Rose*, pp. 100–03; *Syracuse Herald*, October 7, 1911.
45. Pinkerton, *Spy of the Rebellion*, pp. 252–60.
46. Ibid.
47. Ibid.
48. Horan, *The Pinkertons*, pp. 86–87.
49. Ibid.
50. Ibid.
51. Ross, *Rebel Rose*, pp. 120–23.
52. Ibid.

CHAPTER SIX

OPERATIVE ELLEN

SEVERAL MONTHS BEFORE THE START OF THE CIVIL WAR, KATE WARNE was masquerading as a Southern sympathizer and keeping company with women of refinement and wealth from the South. When war did break out, those women were not afraid to express their support of the Rebels. Some of them were secretly supplying the Confederate forces with information they had acquired using their feminine wiles. Kate was tasked with staying close to opponents of the government who were seeking to overthrow it, and secure proof that secrets were being traded.

For weeks Kate had been monitoring the movements of Mrs. Rose Greenhow, a Southern woman believed to be engaged in corresponding with Rebel authorities and furnishing them with valuable intelligence. By late August 1861, Allan Pinkerton and a handful of his most trusted operatives, including Kate, had compiled enough evidence against Rose that a warrant for her arrest was granted. She was outraged when Pinkerton detective agents invaded her home and began gathering boxes of secret reports, letters, and official, classified documents. She called the agents "uncouth ruffians," and objected to her home being searched.[1]

Pinkerton and his team left none of Rose's possessions intact in their quest to extract all suspicious paperwork. The head- and footboards of all the beds were taken apart, mirrors were separated from their backings, pictures were removed from frames, and cabinets and linen closets were inspected. Coded letters were found in shoes and dress pockets. Among the items found in the kitchen stove were orders from the War Department giving the organizational plan to increase the size of the regular army, a diary containing notes about military operations, and numerous incriminating letters from Union officers willing to trade their allegiance to their country for a romantic interlude with Mrs. Greenhow.[2]

According to Rose's account of the inspection of her house and the seizure of many sensitive letters, the "intrusion was insulting." One of the investigators at the scene complimented her on the "scope and quality" of the material found. It was "the most extensive private correspondence that has ever fallen under my examination," the operative confessed. "There is not a distinguished name in America that is not found here. There is nothing that can come under the charge of treason, but enough

Mrs. Rose Greenhow was a renowned Confederate spy. Kate Warne and other Pinkerton operatives helped bring her career to a halt. COURTESY OF THE LIBRARY OF CONGRESS

to make the government dread and hold Mrs. Greenhow as a most dangerous adversary."[3]

Pinkerton had hoped to keep the arrest quiet, but Rose's eight-year-old daughter made that impossible. After witnessing the operatives foraging through her room and the room of her deceased sister, she raced out the back door of the house, shouting, "Mama's been arrested! Mama's been arrested!" Agents chased after the little girl, but after she climbed a tree, nothing could be done until she decided to come down.[4]

A female detective Rose referred to in her memoirs as "Ellen" searched the suspected spy for vital papers hidden in the folds of her dress, in her gloves, shoes, or hair. Nothing was found. Historians suspect the operative Rose referred to as Ellen was Kate Warne. Kate divided her time between guarding the prisoner and questioning leads that could help the detective agency track and apprehend all members of the Greenhow spy ring. Rose realized quickly that Kate was not someone to be trifled with, and she kept her distance.[5]

In the days to come, several women suspected of being a part of Rose's spy ring were also arrested and kept under lock and key with their leader at her house. The Rebel informer's home was referred to as Fort Greenhow, and newspaper reporters flocked to the house of detention hoping to get a look inside and converse with the prisoners. The January 18, 1862, edition of the *Boston Post* included an article about the home for inmates, and described what it looked like. The article reported that Rose and her daughter had been confined to the upstairs portion of the residence, and that all other guests occupied the downstairs.[6] The article continued:

We were admitted to the parlor of the house, formerly occupied by Mrs. Greenhow. Passing through the door on the left we stood in the apartment alluded to. There were others who had stood here before us, we have no doubt of that—men and women of intelligence and refinement. There was a bright fire glowing on the hearth, and a tête-à-tête [an S-shaped sofa on which two people sit face-to-face] was drawn up in front. The two parlors were divided by red curtains, and in the backroom stood a handsome rosewood piano with pearl keys upon which the prisoners of the house, Mrs. G. and her friends, had often performed.[7]

The walls of the room were decorated with portraits of friends and others, some on earth and some in heaven, one of them representing a former daughter of Mrs. Greenhow, Gertrude, a girl of seventeen or eighteen summers, with auburn hair and light blue eyes, who died sometime since.[8]

Just now, as we are examining pictures, there is a noise heard overhead, hardly a noise, for it is the voice of a child, soft and musical. "That is Rosey Greenhow, the daughter of Mrs. Greenhow, playing with the guard," said the Lieutenant, who noticed our inquisitive expression. "It is a strange sound here; you don't often hear it, for it is generally quiet." And then the handsome face of the Lieutenant relaxed into a shade of sadness.

There are many prisoners here, no doubt of that, and maybe the tones of this young child have dropped like rains of spring upon the leaves of the drooping flowers! A moment more and all is quiet, and save the stepping of the guard above there is nothing heard.[9]

Among the number of items seized at the Greenhow home was a cipher or special code used to write cryptic messages. Pinkerton gave the cipher to Kate and asked her to rewrite one of Rose's dispatches and insert bogus information. The dispatch would then be disseminated in hopes of reaching Confederate colonel Thomas Jordan, a key figure in the network of spies. Rose was his protégé, and prior to the First Battle of Bull Run, he had assisted in passing messages about troop numbers and positions. He had devised the cipher Rose used, and Pinkerton believed there was a chance Colonel Jordan would act on the misinformation Kate supplied.[10]

Colonel Jordan was aware that Rose was under house arrest, and considered the possibility that she might have been able to smuggle the message out to him from where she was being held. After examining the letter and discussing the situation with his associates, it was decided that it was too dangerous to reply to her or act on the instructions she suggested. Colonel Jordan created a new cipher and waited. If Rose was still an active informant, the cipher would find its way to her.[11]

Pinkerton was furious that the message Kate had penned had obviously not been deemed legitimate. "Our efforts failed, and I'm sure she expected that," Pinkerton recalled of Rose and her accomplishments as a counterspy. He continued:

She made use of whomever and whatever she could as mediums to carry into effect her unholy purposes . . . She has not used her powers in vain among the officers of the army, not a few of whom she has robbed of patriotic hearts and transformed them into sympathizers with the enemies of the country which had made them all they were . . .[12]

For a great many years Mrs. Greenhow has been the instrument of the very men who now lead in the Rebel councils and some of those who command their armies; who have successfully used her as a willing instrument in plotting the overthrow of the United States Government and which she, no less than they, had desired to accomplish; and since the commencement of this rebellion this woman with her uncommon social powers, her very extensive acquaintance among and her active association with the leading politicians of this nation, has possessed an almost superhuman power, all of which she has most wickedly used to destroy the government. With her as with other traitors, she has been most unscrupulous in the use of means. Nothing has been too sacred for her appropriation, as by its use she might hope to accomplish her treasonable ends.[13]

The fact that Pinkerton and his operatives, as well as Union soldiers, were standing guard inside and outside of Rose's house did not deter her from attempting to get messages to Jefferson Davis. She tried to slip messages out in hollowed-out tobacco plugs and canes. She even placed a note inside a ball of pink yarn and gave the ball to her daughter to deliver. Rose's defiance prompted Pinkerton to have her transferred to the Old Capitol Prison. When rumor reached her that in all probability she would be moved and tried for treason, she boldly announced there would be "rich revelations" if such a thing occurred.[14]

The day Rose was transferred to the Old Capitol Prison, the street where she lived was filled with curious bystanders. Neighbors, business owners, soldiers, and Union supporters lined the thoroughfare to watch the spy being escorted to jail. Kate and the other Pinkerton detectives were on hand to witness Rose's journey as well. Taking her daughter's hand and holding it tightly, she paraded past the sea of faces staring intently at her. Her head up and her eyes fixed straight ahead, Rose said nothing as she walked along. Mother and daughter were housed in a room on the second floor of the prison. Their room had one window overlooking the yard where inmates could congregate. The furnishings were plain: a bed, chair, mirror, and sewing machine.[15]

Rose Greenhow didn't lack contact with the outside world while interned at the Old Capitol Prison. The October 7, 1911, edition of the *Syracuse Herald* noted that there were a number of men and women who delighted in supplying her with any information they had. She also had friends in governmental departments who lost no opportunity in communicating with her. Many letters Rose wrote were to officials she believed could do something about her dismal "living conditions."[16]

"She composed letters of complaint to Congressmen and local authorities," the *Syracuse Herald* reported. "Two of the scathing letters were sent to the Secretary of State and duplicates were successfully dispatched to Richmond, where they were published in the newspapers." According to the January 9, 1862, edition of the *McArthur Democrat*, Rose objected to being a "closed prisoner, shut out from air and exercise."[17] In a complaint to Secretary Seward, she wrote:

> *Patience is said to be a great virtue, and I have practiced it to my utmost capacity of endurance. I am told, sir, that upon your ipse dixit [a dogmatic and unapproved statement] the fate of citizens depends, and that the signed manual of the ministers of Louis XIV and XV had not more potential in their day than that of the Secretary of State in 1861.[18]*
>
> *I therefore most respectfully submit that on Friday, August 23, 1861, without warrant or show of authority, I was arrested by the detective police, and my house taken in charge by them; that all my private letters and papers of a lifetime were read by them; that every law of decency was violated in the search of my house by Pinkerton*

*detectives, and my person by an uncivilized female operative, and by
their surveillance over me.[19]*

Historians suspect that Rose's "uncivilized female operative" refers
to Kate Warne. Rose's letter of grievance to Secretary Seward continued:

*We read in history that the poor Marie Antoinette had a paper torn
from her bosom by lawless hands, and that even a change of linen had
to be affected in sight of her brutal captors. It is my sad experience to
record even more revolting outrages than that, for during the first
days of my imprisonment, whenever necessity forced me to seek my
chamber, a detective stood sentinel at the open door.[20]*

*For a period of time I, with my little child, was placed absolutely
at the mercy of men without character or responsibility; that during
the first evening, a portion of these men became brutally drunk and
boasted in my hearing of the "nice times" they expected to have with
the female prisoners.*

Pinkerton and his operatives utilized the time Rose was incarcerated
to complete their investigation. The additional dispatches collected at the
Greenhow home provided the agents with the names and locations of
key members of her spy network. More than fifteen arrests were made
subsequent to Rose being apprehended.[21]

Eugenia Phillips, the wife of a farmer, Alabama congressman, and
Washington attorney; Colonel Thomas Marshal Key, judge advocate
and McClellan's aide-de-camp; banker William Smithson; and a well-
respected dentist named Aaron Van Camp were among those whom
Pinkerton agents investigated. Their investigation unearthed proof that
supported the premise that the suspects were involved with Rose Greenhow and helped to steal secrets.[22]

Members of the Greenhow spy ring joined Rose in her opinion that
the Pinkerton operatives were manufacturing evidence. Critics of the
detective agency believed they had concocted tales of spies and assassination plots to further their business. Rose's letter-writing campaign
to the secretary of war not only called into question the integrity of the

Pinkerton agency and its operatives, but also included a list of additional problems about life at the Old Capitol Prison. Rose wrote that she was living in a "squalid physical environment, contending with rats, bad food, and exposed to an uncomfortable and unsanitary cell."[23]

The October 7, 1911, *Syracuse Herald* noted that Rose was not so much concerned for herself but for her daughter. "I am seriously alarmed about the health and life of my child. Day by day I see her fading away. Her round chubby face, [formerly] radiant with health, has become as pale as marble. The pupils of her eyes are unnaturally dilated, and finally, a slow, nervous fever seized upon her. I implored in vain, both verbally and in writing, that a physician might be sent."[24]

Rose declined the services of a military doctor called to the prison. She wrote the provost marshal and told him that the treatment of her child had no "precedent in a civilized age." In response to her note, a doctor was sent whose services she had already rejected. Rose tossed the doctor out of the cell. Finally, her family physician was allowed to examine the girl. With better food and more exercise, the child's health improved.[25]

The hearing against Rose Greenhow began in March 1862. She considered the entire proceeding an outrage. She wasted no time in proclaiming it a mock trial, scoffing at the incriminating evidence compiled by Pinkerton and his Washington operatives. She referred to all the detectives as "despicable scoundrels," and "denied any wrongdoing." "I have not made nor will I make any confession of treason or treasonable correspondence," Rose announced to the court on April 2, 1862. "Neither was I subjected to an examination intended to bring to the light my sources of information. I but claim the right which our fathers did in '76—to protest against tyranny and oppression."[26]

Rose Greenhow was found guilty of being a spy against the federal government and was sentenced to be banished from the North. On June 2, 1862, Rose, her daughter, and four other female traitors were released from the Old Capitol Prison and sent to Baltimore. From there the women were to be transported by boat to the South. The June 3, 1862, edition of the *National Republican* reported that Rose received "quite an ovation from the secession women of Baltimore, much to the disgust of the Union people of the city."[27]

Pinkerton objected to Rose and the other accused traitors being exiled and transported to the South. His operatives had been seen by Rose, and Pinkerton feared that if she was permitted to travel to Richmond (where she requested to be sent), she would expose the detectives and their lives would be in jeopardy. She could provide the Rebels with descriptions of George Bangs and Kate Warne. Both agents worked assignments throughout the Confederate states, and if they were recognized as detectives employed by the Union, they would be put to death. Pinkerton believed Rose should have been hanged for her actions and not allowed to place the lives of his best operatives at such risk.[28]

Rose was celebrated in Richmond. Jefferson Davis, president of the Confederate States, extended his appreciation for her patriotism. According to Rose's memoirs, Davis boasted that there would have been no victory at the first Bull Run without her help.[29]

If the efforts of operatives like Kate Warne and Hattie Lawton had been made public, perhaps the press would have praised the capable agents for their work at uncovering Rebel espionage rings. The women employed by the Pinkerton Detective Agency were content with being anonymous. They lived their lives in secret; apart from exposure to counterspies such as Rose Greenhow, there was little chance of their vocation being discovered. As long as Rose was free, Pinkerton operatives would be on guard.[30]

When Rose left the country with her daughter in August 1863, she hadn't a worry in the world. She was headed to London to write a book about her experiences as a spy imprisoned by Union forces, Allan Pinkerton, and his agents. The book, entitled *My Imprisonment and the First Year of Abolition Rule at Washington*, became a bestseller. In August 1864, Rose returned to America aboard the steamer *Condor*, leaving her daughter behind in France. Parisian convent school. She was carrying with her the proceeds she had earned from the sale of her book, hundreds of gold sovereigns sewn into her corset and underclothes.[31]

On the evening of September 30, 1864, the *Condor* was making its way from Halifax, Nova Scotia, Canada, when it entered the New Inlet Bar near Wilmington, North Carolina. In the dark of the night, the captain of the vessel mistook a partially sunken blockade ship as a working ship set to attack. Hoping to avoid a collision, the captain turned the *Condor* out of the way and accidentally ran the vessel aground. Rose and two Confederate agents decided to escape from the doomed ship using lifeboats. The lifeboats quickly overturned in the rough water. Rose was attempting to swim ashore when she drowned, the gold sovereigns she was wearing having weighed her down.[32]

Newspapers throughout the South reported on Rose's death, as well as the particulars of her funeral. The October 20, 1864, *Wilmington Journal* noted that "hundreds of ladies lined the wharf at Wilmington upon the approach of Mrs. Greenhow's remains." The Soldiers' Aid Society took charge of the funeral, held in the chapel of Hospital No. 4. "It was a solemn and imposing spectacle," the *Wilmington Journal* article continued. "Mrs. Greenhow leaves one child, an interesting little daughter, who is in convent school at Paris, where her mother left her upon her return to this country."[33]

Among the items found on Rose's body was a copy of her book, a note to her daughter, and a cipher that provided a key to the messages she had sent to Confederate commanders.[34]

As head of the Secret Service for the Union Army, Allan Pinkerton was called on to recruit agents with varying skills. In addition to ships' officers, farmers, merchants, and clerks, he hired seamstresses, socialites, and, in the case of Vinnie Ream, an artist. From the time Lincoln was elected president and the Baltimore plot was uncovered, Pinkerton was dedicated to the protection of the Great Emancipator. Rumors of plans to assassinate President Lincoln were consistently brought to the detective's attention, and he was honor-bound to investigate every report.[35]

Some of the threats to do away with the president were believed to have originated from within Mr. Lincoln's own administration. In order to discover which politician might be plotting against the leader, Pinkerton needed to enlist the help of individuals who could get inside the operation without raising suspicions. An American sculptor commissioned to make a marble statue of President Lincoln was drafted by Pinkerton as one of those inside the operation.[36]

Vinnie Ream was just seventeen years old in 1864 when the president agreed to model for her. Creating the bust of his figure would take six months. The Wisconsin native was a gifted artist who apprenticed with sculptor Clark Mills in Washington. Mills was highly respected, and had been commissioned by Congress in 1853 to create a statue of Andrew Jackson on a horse.[37]

Prior to Vinnie being able to utilize her artistic talent for President Lincoln, she was working at the dead letter office of the United States

While sculpting Lincoln's bust at the White House, artist Vinnie Ream had the opportunity to overhear important information to aid Allen Pinkerton with his work protecting the President. COURTESY OF THE LIBRARY OF CONGRESS

Post Office. She was one of the first women to be employed by the federal government. Because Pinkerton was Scottish he believed Vinnie, who was also from Scottish ancestry, would be the perfect undercover agent.[38]

President Lincoln was poised to be reelected for a second term, and those vehemently and violently opposed to the idea were planning to kidnap him and hold him ransom for the release of Confederate prisoners languishing in Northern jails. Vinnie's job was to report to Pinkerton any information she could acquire about potential conspirators in the White House.[39]

During the time Vinnie was creating the sculpture, senators and congressmen filtered in and out of the crypt in the Capitol where she was working to watch the process. She had opportunity to overhear conversations between politicians and staff that were not for public consumption. She was instructed to inform Pinkerton of any suspicious activity or talk against President Lincoln's policies from his Cabinet, in particular, Vice President Andrew Johnson.[40]

Exactly what Vinnie shared with Pinkerton is not known, but members of the Radical Republicans (a faction of the Republican Party who were proslavery, and thus, opposed to Mr. Lincoln) believed she had significant political influence. After President Lincoln was assassinated in April 1865, and Andrew Johnson was sworn in as president, members of the Radical Republicans who knew of Vinnie's association with Allan Pinkerton called upon her to assist them in helping to ensure Johnson's impeachment.[41]

According to the February 23, 1868, edition of the *Detroit Free Press*,

The impeachment of President Andrew Johnson arose from uncompromised beliefs and a contest for power in a nation struggling with reunification. Before President Lincoln was killed his plan of reconstruction called for leniency toward the South as it rejoined the Union. He planned to grant a general amnesty to those who pledged an oath of loyalty to the United States and agreed to obey all federal laws pertaining to slavery. Andrew Johnson was intent on carrying out his plan when he took office. The idea didn't sit well with the Radical Republicans, and they organized an effort to impeach Johnson.[42]

Influential members of the Radical Republicans, like US senator Charles Sumner and representative Thaddeus Stevens, threatened to expose Vinnie as a Pinkerton operative if she didn't help to persuade Senator Edmund Ross (a friend of the Ream family) to vote in favor of impeaching Johnson. "The vote of Senator Ross of Kansas was needed to help secure a unanimous vote of Johnson's impeachment," an article in the September 22, 1907, *Des Moines Register* noted, "and the Radical Republicans tried to get the sculptress to influence him." She refused.

The men then asked her to give them access to her home, where Ross was living at the time, so they could speak with him personally about the matter. She reluctantly consented, but when the politicians arrived at the house, Vinnie "placed herself in their path and would not allow them to pass."[43]

On Friday, February 24, 1868, Congress voted to impeach President Andrew Johnson. The February 29, 1868, edition of the *Warren Mail* reported that the "bold, bad man and accidental President's fate had been sealed." The article went on to explain that "after an able discussion impeachment was passed by a vote of one-hundred-twenty-six yays [*sic*] to forty-seven nays." As a penance for defying the Radical Republicans, Vinnie was nearly thrown out of the Capitol, but the intervention of powerful, influential New York sculptors prevented anything serious from happening to her.[44]

The white marble statue Vinnie Ream sculpted of President Abraham Lincoln was unveiled in the US Capitol rotunda on January 25, 1871. The January 29, 1871, *Harrisburg Telegraph* noted that among the government leaders present were associate justices Davis and Clifford, the secretary of the interior, and several members of the Illinois congressional delegation. Mr. Lincoln was presented as holding in his hand the Emancipation Proclamation.[45]

Vinnie died at her home in Washington, DC, on November 20, 1914, after suffering from a long illness. Pinkerton called on the artist in 1875 when she sculpted a bust of George Custer, and in 1878, after she received a commission to sculpt Admiral David G. Farragut. What they discussed at either occasion is not known.[46]

Absolute discretion was one of Vinnie's most admirable qualities. She never elaborated on her role with the Pinkerton Agency, even in the memoirs she wrote and privately distributed in 1908. Neither is there any reference to the Pinkerton Agency in any of her biographies. She seems to have taken the secret of their association to her grave.

Notes

1. Winkler, *Stealing Secrets*, p. 17; Ross, *Rebel Rose*, pp. 117–20.
2. Winkler, *Stealing Secrets*, pp. 15–16; Pinkerton, *Spy of the Rebellion*, pp. 251–53.
3. Ross, *Rebel Rose*, pp. 135–36; Winkler, *Stealing Secrets*, pp. 17–18.
4. Winkler, *Stealing Secrets*, pp. 14–15.
5. Winkler, *Stealing Secrets*, pp. 17–18; Ross, *Rebel Rose*, pp. 135–36.
6. *Boston Post*, January 18, 1862.
7. Horan, *The Pinkertons*, pp. 87–88; Pinkerton, *Spy of the Rebellion*, pp. 188–90; Ross, *Rebel Rose*, pp. 22–23.
8. Ibid.
9. Ibid.
10. Horan, *The Pinkertons*, pp. 88–89; Winkler, *Stealing Secrets*, pp. 16–17.
11. Winkler, *Stealing Secrets*, pp. 11–16, 26–27; Moran, *The Eye That Never Sleeps*, 43–44.
12. Ross, *Rebel Rose*, pp. 142–45.
13. Ross, *Rebel Rose*, pp. 142–45; Horan, *The Pinkertons*, pp. 88–89.
14. Ross, *Rebel Rose*, pp. 142–45; Winkler, *Stealing Secrets*, pp. 18–20.
15. Winkler, *Stealing Secrets*, pp. 18–20; Ross, *Rebel Rose*, pp. 145–47.
16. *Syracuse Herald*, October 7, 1911.
17. *Syracuse Herald*, October 7, 1911; *McArthur Democrat*, January 9, 1862.
18. *McArthur Democrat*, January 9, 1862.
19. Ibid.
20. Ross, *Rebel Rose*, pp. 157–59.
21. Horan, *The Pinkertons*, pp. 94–95.
22. Winkler, *Stealing Secrets*, pp. 19–20; *The Magnet, Agriculture Commercial, and Family Gazette*, July 13, 1868.
23. Winkler, *Stealing Secrets*, pp. 19–20.
24. *Syracuse Herald*, October 7, 1911; Ross, *Rebel Rose*, pp. 164–66.
25. Winkler, *Stealing Secrets*, pp. 22–24; *Syracuse Herald*, October 7, 1911.
26. Ross, *Rebel Rose*, pp. 192–93; Horan, *The Pinkertons*, pp. 94–95.
27. *National Republican*, June 3, 1862.
28. Horan, *The Pinkertons*, pp. 94–96.
29. Ross, *Rebel Rose*, pp. 201–04.
30. Winkler, *Stealing Secrets*, pp. 25–26.
31. Winkler, *Stealing Secrets*, pp. 25–26; Horan, *The Pinkertons*, pp. 96–97; Ross, *Rebel Rose*, pp. 219–21.
32. Ross, *Rebel Rose*, pp. 219–21; Winkler, *Stealing Secrets*, pp. 25–27.

33. *Wilmington Journal*, October 20, 1864.

34. Winkler, *Stealing Secrets*, p. 27; *Richmond Dispatch*, October 8, 1864.

35. *Chronicle-Telegram*, January 3, 1882.

36. Horan, *The Pinkertons*, pp. 36, 54–55.

37. *New York Times*, January 27, 1853; *Sculpting Lincoln*, pp. 78–101.

38. Cooper, *Vinnie Ream: An American Sculptor*, pp. 3, 7–11.

39. Emerson, *Giant in the Shadows*, pp. 280–81; *The Rail Splitter: A Journal for the Lincoln Collector* (Fall 2000).

40. *Des Moines Register*, September 22, 1951.

41. Trefousse, *Historical Dictionary of Reconstruction*, pp. 175–76.

42. *Detroit Free Press*, February 23, 1868.

43. *Des Moines Register*, September 22, 1907.

44. *Warren Mail*, February 29, 1868.

45. *Harrisburg Telegraph*, January 29, 1871; *Sculpting Lincoln*, pp. 78–101; Cooper, *Vinnie Ream: An American Sculptor*, pp. 15–17.

46. *Washington Post*, July 13, 1982.

CHAPTER SEVEN

OPERATIVES ELIZABETH BAKER AND MARY TOUVESTRE

ELIZABETH BAKER SAT AT A SMALL BURLED WALNUT DESK, FRANTI-cally scribbling on thick sheets of paper. A silhouette of her image cast on the fabric-covered walls showed her flipping through the sheets of paper. She was inspecting a variety of crude drawings of ships. The flame from a lit candle on the desk next to her danced in harmony with a draft seeping in through a closed window. It was early fall of 1861 in Richmond, Virginia. The Civil War was in its infancy, and military leaders from the North and South had sent spies behind enemy lines to learn whatever secrets they could.

Allan Pinkerton directed Mrs. Elizabeth H. Baker to go to the Confederate capital to acquire information about the Rebel navy. She didn't hesitate to abide by the detective's orders. Elizabeth had been working as an operative for the Pinkerton Detective Agency for a number of years. Although assigned to the Chicago office, she had traveled out of town on occasion, teaming with other agents to investigate robberies and missing person cases. Prior to moving to the Midwest, she had lived in Virginia and was well acquainted with the customs and the people of the region. When war broke out she relocated. Pinkerton referred to her as a "genteel woman agent," and considered her "a more than suitable" candidate for the assignment he'd selected for her.[1]

Elizabeth wrote two sets of friends she had known from her days living in Richmond and informed them of her plans to visit. Claiming to miss being in Virginia, she told them she wanted to return and stay for a long visit. As luck would have it, Captain Atwater of the Confederate Navy and his wife invited Elizabeth to stay with them when she came to Richmond.[2]

Elizabeth arrived at the Atwaters' home on September 24, 1861. The reunion was a happy one, and the three friends attended numerous receptions, balls, and fund-raisers together. Elizabeth met influential socialites, Confederate officers, and politically ambitious Southerners who claimed to possess the precise plans needed to defeat the North.[3]

Drinks flowed at many of the soirees the Atwaters and Elizabeth were invited to attend. Tongues loosened as champagne and bourbon were consumed. One evening, after having too much to drink, Elizabeth's host decided to discuss the issues between the states and speculated on the tactics the Confederate Navy would use to ensure that the South would win the war. Elizabeth played her part well, agreeing with Captain Atwater about the North's weaknesses and how much better life would be when the South defeated the Yankees.[4]

When the three friends were not attending grand social functions, they were touring the city. Elizabeth made mental note of the number of Confederate forces amassing in Richmond, the artillery being transported in and out of the city, and the fortifications being built around it. In the evenings before retiring to bed, Elizabeth jotted down everything she had seen and sketched the vital information on scraps of paper. She hid the notes and sketches in the crown of her bonnet.[5]

One morning in late September, Captain Atwater made mention that part of his workday would be spent watching the demonstration of an unnamed submarine vessel referred to as the *Cheney*, a two-man underwater vessel built by William Cheney. Elizabeth casually expressed an interest in seeing the demonstration, and Captain Atwater agreed that she and his wife could accompany him. "If you and Mrs. Atwater will be ready by nine o'clock," the captain told Elizabeth, "we will have ample time to reach the place, which is some few miles below the city."[6]

Elizabeth contained her enthusiasm at the announcement. This was the exact area of warfare that Pinkerton had instructed her to learn more about. The detectives had heard rumors that the Confederates were developing torpedoes and submarine vessels to battle against Union blockades.[7]

According to the September 25, 1861, edition of the *Janesville Daily Gazette*, the submarine in question was "shaped like a cigar, drawing thirteen feet of water, while only seven are above the surface." The article went on to note that "it was one hundred five feet long, covered with thick, iron plates, with spikes at the bow and the stern. This vessel cannot only break through blockades, but sink them." The exhibition of the vessel was to take place in the James River. Designed by William L. Cheney, a New York–born former US Navy officer who later joined the Confederate Navy, the submarine held a crew of two or three men. Captain Atwater explained to Elizabeth that the vessel was operated using a series of gears and levers. She was also told the sub was "but a small working model of a much larger one; it would be finished in two weeks."[8]

Elizabeth carefully watched the submarine and the crew through a pair of field glasses Captain Atwater gave her. She was informed that the men inside the vessel wore diving armor which enabled them to work underwater. The air they breathed was supplied from a hose affixed to a sea-green floatation collar that rested on top of the water behind the submarine. Additional hoses were used by divers venturing outside the submarine. Divers worked underwater, attaching a torpedo to the ship they intended to blow up.[9]

Elizabeth witnessed a scow (a flat-bottomed boat with a front bow, often used to haul bulk freight) being towed into the river and anchored several miles out from the docks. The submarine then set off after the vessel. The location of the underwater boat was easy to follow because of the floating collar. When the submarine reached a designated spot, divers carrying magazines or torpedo canisters were offloaded and swam to the target. The divers then attached the explosives to the scow and ventured back to the submarine. Once inside, the vessel backed away from the target (as evidenced by the movement of the floating collar), and moments later, the scow exploded.[10]

The crowd watching the boat being blown to bits cheered and applauded. "Without any previous warning there was a concussion from the blast and it took us aback," Elizabeth later wrote in her report to

Pinkerton. "The scow seemed to be lifted bodily out of the water and thrown into the air. Her destruction was complete." Captain Atwater explained to her that the larger submarine the Confederates would use on the North was specifically earmarked to protect steamers *Patrick Henry* and *Thomas Jefferson*. Both steamers would be leaving Norfolk, Virginia, soon, loaded with cotton and bound for England. It was imperative that they reach their destination. Elizabeth was told that the name of the submarine that would see the steamers through was called the *Merrimack*.[11]

The *Merrimack* was a frigate, best known as the hull upon which the ironclad warship the CSS *Virginia* was constructed. Built and launched in 1855, she was decommissioned in 1860 after traveling through the Caribbean, Western Europe, and Central America. The *Merrimack* sat at the Norfolk Navy Shipyard until April 1861. The Confederacy, in desperate need of ships, decided to rebuild the frigate as an ironclad.[12]

The October 5, 1861, edition of the *Emporia Weekly News* carried an article about the activity of the Confederate Navy and its plans for the *Merrimack*. The article also included news about the general condition of the Southern capital:

> *Dr. Wilson, Surgeon in the United States Army, and taken prisoner at Bull Run by the Rebels, was released on parole and reached Rich-mond. He says there is great distress and dissatisfaction in the Rebel capitol. All the hotels are fitted up as hospitals, and are filled with sick and wounded. There are four hundred men of the Florida regiments in the hospitals. Medicines of all kinds are costly. Quinine sells at eight dollars an ounce and is very scarce.[13]*
>
> *All the necessaries of life are dear. Small change is very scarce. Confederate currency is depreciating, the best commanding 15 percent premium. All the physicians of the city agree that there are at least two thousand influential citizens of Richmond that do not believe an attack will be made on Washington. Beauregard's headquarters are at Fairfax Court House. Johnson's headquarters are near Winchester. There are about four thousand troops at Norfolk. At the latter place the Rebels are converting the steamer* Merrimack *into a floating battery.[14]*

Pinkerton was made aware of the article in the *Emporia Weekly News* and shared the information with Major General George B. McClellan. The two men looked forward to hearing from Elizabeth, hoping for more-detailed news about the Confederate Navy's activities. She had every intention of reporting her findings to Pinkerton, but not before she'd had a chance to visit the Tredegar Iron Works, the primary iron and artillery production facility in the South. Before Elizabeth had made it back to the Atwaters' after the submarine demonstration, the captain had invited his wife and their guest to tour the facility.[15]

The massive munitions factory was the largest of its kind in the South. The Tredegar Iron Works supplied half of the South's total domestic production of artillery, including giant, rail-mounted siege cannons, steam locomotives, and iron plating for the ironclad warships. Elizabeth saw two submarines being constructed as she walked through the facility. Captain Atwater told her that the vessels would be completed and in the water by November.[16]

The October 21, 1861, edition of the *Fayetteville Weekly Observer* reported that the Tredegar Iron Works would prove to be the key to the South winning the war:

> *There are more than fifteen hundred men employed at the Iron Works. They turn over ten cannons per day from five- to one-hundred-and-thirty-four-pounders; Columbiads, howitzers, field pieces, rifles, shells, and shot and balls enough to supply an army of five hundred thousand men. The capacity of the establishment is immense, and is essential for the Confederacy to reign victorious.*[17]

Elizabeth was frantic to get the news of what was being produced at the factory and the capabilities of submarines to Pinkerton. "Unless something was done, and quickly," she would inform Pinkerton, "untold disaster would attend the Union cause."[18]

Captain Atwater escorted Elizabeth and his wife home, and that evening Elizabeth was busy drawing what she'd seen at the iron works, along with the submarines, floats, and ships moored at the location on the James River.[19] Pinkerton noted Elizabeth's actions in his report:

Operative Elizabeth Baker's tour of the Tredegar Iron Works facility in Richmond, Virginia, proved to be life-saving for Union soldiers. COURTESY OF THE LIBRARY OF CONGRESS

The next day, being Sunday, she remained at the residence of the Captain. On Monday morning, having procured a pass, she bade farewell to her host and his amiable spouse, and left Richmond for Fredericksburg. From thence she made her way to Washington, and lost no time in reporting to me the success of her trip. She had made a hasty, though quite comprehensive, sketch of the vessel, which showed the position under the surface of the water and explained its workings.[20]

Pinkerton wasted no time in submitting the information to General McClellan and the secretary of the navy. The officers forwarded the intelligence on to the commanders of the squadrons, instructing them to keep a careful eye peeled for float collars, and to drag the water for the purposes of grabbing the air hoses connecting the float with the vessel below. The US Navy used the intelligence collected to enhance their antisubmarine measures, which, until this point, had consisted of nets weighted down with chains hung around the ships. These crude items were used to keep any submarine from getting close enough to attach explosives to destroy the ships.[21] Remarked Pinkerton in his writings:

Nothing was heard about locating collars or vessels for weeks after Elizabeth's information was delivered. Then came the day I was

informed that one of the vessels of the blockading fleet off the mouth of the James River had discovered the float, and putting out her drag-rope, had caught the air-tubes and thus effectively disabled the vessel from doing any harm, and no doubt drowning all who were on board of her.[22]

This incident, and the peculiarity of the machine, was discussed in the newspapers at that time, who stated that "by a mere accident the Federal fleet off James River had been saved from destruction," but I knew much better, and that the real credit of the discovery was due to a lady of my own force.[23]

The information Elizabeth was able to acquire helped in another wartime incident known as the Battle of Hampton Roads, occurring March 8 and 9, 1862. The March 31, 1862, edition of the *Fayetteville Weekly Observer* reported about the conflict:

About eleven o'clock a dark looking object was described coming around Craney Island through Norfolk channel, and proceeded straight in our direction. As she came ploughing through the water onward toward the port she looked like a huge half submerged crocodile. Her sides seemed of solid iron, except where the guns pointed from the narrow ports, and rose slantingly from the water like the roof of a house or the arched back of a tortoise.[24]

At her prow one could see the iron projecting straight forward, somewhat above the water's edge, and apparently a mass of iron. Small boats were strung or fastened to her sides, and the Confederate flag floated from one staff while a pennant was fixed to another at the stern. There was a smoke stack or pipe near her middle, and she was probably a propeller, no side wheels or machinery being visible. She was probably covered with railroad iron.[25]

We fired constantly, and the Merrimack *occasionally, but every shot told upon our wooden vessel and brave crew. Her guns being without the least elevation, pointed straight at us along the surface of the water, and her nearness, she being much of the time within three hundred yards, made it an easy matter to send each ball to its exact mark. Probably her guns would be useless at a considerable distance, as it appears impossible to elevate them.*[26]

Immediately on the appearing of the Merrimack *the command was given by the Union officers to make ready for instant action. All hands were ordered to their places, and the* Cumberland *was sprung across the channel, so that her broadside would bear on the* Merrimack. *When the* Merrimack *arrived within about a mile, we opened on her with our pivot guns, and as soon as we could bear upon her, our whole broadside commenced. Still she came on, the balls bouncing from her sides like India rubber, apparently making not the least impression, except to cut off her flag-staff, and thus bring down the Confederate colors.*[27]

It was impossible for our vessel to get out of her way, and the Merrimack *soon crashed her iron horn or ram into the* Cumberland *just starboard the main chains, under the bluff of the port bow, knocking a hole in the side near the waterline, as large as the head of a hogshead and driving the vessel back upon her anchors with great force. The water came rushing into the hole. The* Merrimack *then backed out and discharged her guns at us, the shot passing through the main bay and killing five sick men.*[28]

And then there was the Monitor *which fired 178-pound cast-iron shot. The wrought-iron shot was not used, because their great weight and peculiar construction render the guns much more liable to burst. The* Merrimack *fired about forty shots on the* Monitor, *which replied as rapidly as possible; but so far as is known, neither vessel is damaged. Those on board on the* Monitor *say the balls rattled and ran upon both vessels and seemed to bounce off harmless.*[29]

The fight between the Monitor *and the* Merrimack *continued, and they eventually arrived side by side and engaged one another for four hours and twenty minutes. Once the* Merrimack *dashed her iron prow quarterly against the* Monitor *but did not injure that vessel in the least. The* Monitor *in turn determined to try her force in a similar operation, but in some unaccountable manner the wheel or other steering apparatus became entangled, it is said, and the* Monitor *rushed by, just missing her arm. In the end the* Monitor *was victorious.*[30]

The efficient manner in which this work was performed was of great service to the nation, and sustained the reputation of the Secret Service Department, as being an important adjunct in aiding the government in its efforts to suppress the rebellion.[31]

While operative Baker was visiting the factory where Confederate submarines were being built, another operative was working on acquiring a set of plans for the rebuilding of the steamer *Merrimack*. Free slave Mary Touvestre (some historical accounts list her name as Louvestre) was employed as a seamstress and housekeeper for one of the Rebel engineers restoring the steam-powered frigate. She overheard the engineer discussing the importance of the vessel as a weapon against the Union, and decided to offer her services to her country. Her association with Pinkerton was through Secretary of the Navy Gideon Welles.[32]

With the help of civilian railroad builder William Mahone, the Gosport Shipyard in Portsmouth, Virginia, was captured by Confederate forces in April 1861. A substantial volume of war materiel was seized in the process, including more than a thousand heavy guns and the US Navy ship, the *Merrimack*. Union forces tried to sink the ironclad rather than let her fall into Rebel hands, but she did not go down all the way. The ship's lower hull and machinery were intact. The Confederate Navy managed to raise the ship out of the water and began making plans to rebuild her.[33]

According to the June 19, 1861, edition of the *Times-Picayune*, there was a great deal of confidence in her ability to join the fight for the South. The article noted:

The Merrimack *has gotten up, and repairs are to be made on her forthwith. The Lincolnites burned this noble frigate down to the copper. Two or three months, however, will suffice to make her whole again. Three or four steamers are being fitted out at the Navy Yard, after the man-of-war style, to cruise in the sounds of North Carolina and to run out to sea and pick up the merchant marine of the North. This will be glorious fun, and the gallant officers who command these vessels will doubtless reap a rich harvest from the Yankee Doodles.*[34]

Mary Touvestre overheard several conversations about the frigate turned ironclad which was being renamed the CSS *Virginia*. She heard that the "steamer was being turned into a floating battery," and that it was "shot-proof." Rumor had it that the only way to prevent the vessel from leaving Norfolk was to fill the mouth of the Elizabeth River with heavy blocks of granite.[35]

The CSS *Virginia*, with more than forty guns on either side of the vessel, posed a major threat to Northern blockades. Mary saw the gravity of the situation and sought to intervene. The engineer she worked for brought the plans for the ship home with him nightly. Mary decided she would steal the plans and turn them over to Union forces. In late September 1861, she sewed the vital information into the hem of her dress and set out for Washington.[36]

The journey from Portsmouth, Virginia, to the federal capital was more than 190 miles. Mary made the trip on foot. When she arrived in Washington, she immediately set out to meet with the secretary of the navy. Secreting the plans out of Virginia past enemy lines was difficult enough, but gaining an audience with a high-ranking military official also proved to have its challenges. Mary had to talk her way around members of Secretary Welles's staff in order to see him. When Mary was finally able to speak with Welles, she explained where she had come from, and presented him with the plans for the ironclad, CSS *Virginia*. The secretary commended Mary's bravery and dedication; had she been captured by the Confederates, she surely would have been put to death.[37]

In reviewing the plans, Secretary Welles and his staff learned that the CSS *Virginia* had a seven-inch, pivot-mounted rifle at each end of the ship and a broadside battery of two six-inch rifles and six nine-inch smooth bores (a gun with an unrifled barrel). Affixed to her bow was an iron ram, allowing the ship herself to be employed as a deadly weapon. Every wooden warship in every navy in the world was totally obsolete against it. The Union was already at work on their own ironclad, the *Monitor*. The information Mary supplied prompted them to speed up production on the vessel.[38]

It was imperative that the Union blockades set in Norfolk and Hampton Roads hold their positions; if not, Confederate ships carrying much-needed supplies from Europe to the South would get through.[39]

Mary remained in Washington and waited for the day there would be news about the CSS *Virginia*. She anticipated that the Rebels would plan a course of action once the engineer realized Mary and the plans were missing.[40]

In early March 1862, word that the USS *Cumberland*—a former patrol ship that was once used to cruise the coast of Africa, with orders to stop vessels carrying slaves—was stationed at the Gosport Navy Yard and commanded to stop any Confederate ship from getting in and out of the area. The USS *Cumberland* was a fifty-gun sailing frigate that had managed to capture several Rebel ships since she had been stationed in Virginia. The USS *Congress* was also a sailing frigate that had served in the Mexican-American War in 1847. More than four hundred sailors were assigned to the vessel.[41]

The March 15, 1862, edition of the *Weekly Sun* described the disaster that occurred to the USS *Cumberland* and USS *Congress*. The *Cumberland* was run down, and the *Congress* was forced to surrender.

About noon today, March 8, the rebel steamship Merrimack *and two gun boats were seen coming around Craney Island headed for Newport News. Half an hour after, the Naval lookout boat in the Roads signalized the fact to the* Minnesota *and* Roanoke, *the latter being the flagships. . . .*[42]

The Merrimack *was making good time for Newport News, where the sailing frigates* Congress *and* Cumberland *were the only naval vessels. As the* Minnesota *passed within range at Sewell's Point, that battery opened on her. Its fire was returned vigorously. The firing being at long range, no perceptible effects were produced. In a little more than one hour from getting under way, the* Merrimack *was now within half a mile from Newport News; the firing commenced. Simultaneously with these movements, the* Yorktown *and* Jamestown *[Rebel steamers] came down the James River, and joined their fire with that of the* Merrimack *upon the* Congress *and the* Cumberland.[43]

The Merrimack *seemed to proceed past the* Congress *and engage the* Cumberland, *which was also under fire of the* Yorktown *and the* Jamestown. *In about half an hour the masts of the* Cumberland, *which were visible over the point of land, were seen to list and finally go over, proving that she had sunk. About that time the* Congress, *with sails spread, was seen to come down a short distance and stop on the Point, apparently aground.*[44]

Soon after, the Merrimack *reappeared and engaged her at short range; and, after keeping up the contest fifteen or twenty minutes, the white flag of surrender was seen to float over the* Congress's *deck.*[45]

The Cumberland *had a crew of five hundred men, nearly one half of whom perished when she went down. As yet, the* Congress *has not been boarded, and it is supposed that soldiers on shore prevented the Rebels from doing so.*[46]

The initial reports about what took place at Hampton Roads were discouraging to Mary, the secretary of the navy, Pinkerton, and every other defender of the Union.

Circumstances changed for the North when the USS *Monitor* arrived at the battle. Six months after Mary had delivered the news to the head of the navy and Pinkerton was subsequently informed, the Federals' ironclad was ready to go to war against the Confederates' ironclad.[47] An article in the March 17, 1862, *Indianapolis Indiana State Sentinel* noted:[48]

Before daylight on Sunday morning [March 9, 1862] the Monitor *moved in and took a position alongside of the* Minnesota, *lying between the* Fortress, *where she could not be seen by the Rebels, but were ready, with steam up, to slip out.*

Up to noon on Sunday the Rebels gave no indication of what were their further designs. The Merrimack *lay up toward Craney Island, in view, but motionless. At one o'clock she was observed in motion, and came out, followed by the* Yorktown *and* Jamestown, *both crowded with troops.*[49]

BATTLE BETWEEN THE MONITOR AND MERRIMAC

Operative Elizabeth Baker uncovered Confederate Navy plans for Ironclads and Operative Mary Touvestre delivered them into the hands of the Union. The Ironclad turned out to be the *Merrimack*. COURTESY OF THE LIBRARY OF CONGRESS

As the Rebel flotilla came out from Sewell's Point, the Monitor *stood out boldly toward them. It is doubtful if the Rebels knew what to make of the strange-looking battery, or if they despised it. Even the* Yorktown *kept on approaching till a thirteen shell from the* Monitor *sent her right about. The* Merrimack *and the* Monitor *kept on approaching each other, the former waiting until she would choose her distance, and the latter apparently not knowing what to make of her funny-looking antagonist.[50]*

The first shot from the Monitor *was fired when about one hundred yards' distance from the* Merrimack, *and the distance was subsequently reduced to fifty yards, and at no time during the two hours of furious cannoning that ensued were the vessels more than two hundred yards apart.[51]*

The officers of the Monitor *at this time had gained such confidence in the impregnability of their battery that they no longer fired at random or hastily. The fight then assumed its more interesting respects. The* Monitor *[ran] around the* Merrimack *repeatedly, probing her sides, looking for her weak points and reserving her fire with a coolness that must have been intensely aggravating for the officer of her enemy, until she had the right spot and exact range, and made her experiments accordingly. In this way the* Merrimack *received three shots which must have seriously damaged her. The first went in about at the smoke stack. The next shot was put low down on her side, near the edge of the iron roofing, which overhangs her sides somewhat like a penthouse. The next shot was placed nearly in the same position. Neither of these shots rebounded at all, but appeared to cut their way through iron and wood into the ship. Soon after receiving the third shot the* Merrimack *turned toward Sewell's Point and made off at full speed.*[52]

The Monitor *followed the* Merrimack *until she got well inside Sewell's Point and then returned to the* Minnesota. *It is probable that the pursuit would have been continued still further, but Lieutenant Worden, her commander, had previously had his eyes injured, and it was also felt that as so much depended on the* Monitor, *it was important not to expose her unnecessarily.*[53]

Historians speculate that if Mary Touvestre had not warned the navy of the Confederate's plans, the *Merrimack* would have been allowed to roam the James River for a longer period of time, and ships from Europe would have been able to reach their Southern destinations with supplies. The outcome of the war might have been different if not for the work of these female spies.[54]

NOTES

1. Pinkerton, *Spy of the Rebellion*, pp. 394–395.
2. Winkler, *Stealing Secrets*, pp. 89–93.
3. Winkler, *Stealing Secrets*, pp. 89–93; Pinkerton, *Spy of the Rebellion*, pp. 247–48.
4. Pinkerton, *Spy of the Rebellion*, pp. 247–48.
5. Ibid.

6. Ibid.
7. Ibid.
8. *Janesville Daily Gazette*, September 25, 1861.
9. Winkler, *Stealing Secrets*, pp. 89–93; Scott, *The War of the Rebellion, 1897*, pp. 401–03.
10. Winkler, *Stealing Secrets*, pp. 89–93; Scott, *The War of the Rebellion, 1897*, pp. 401–03.
11. Chaffin, *The H. L. Hunley*, pp. 59–62; Winkler, *Stealing Secrets*, pp. 89–93; Scott, *The War of the Rebellion, 1897*, pp. 401–03.
12. Silverstone, *Civil War Navies, 1855–1883*, pp. 113–15; Olmsted, *Big Guns: Civil War Siege, Seacoast & Naval Cannon*, pp. 128–30; Chaffin, *The H. L. Hunley*, pp. 59–62; Winkler, *Stealing Secrets*, pp. 89–93; Scott, *The War of the Rebellion, 1897*, pp. 401–03.
13. *Emporia Weekly News*, October 5, 1861.
14. Ibid.
15. Ibid.
16. "Tredegar Iron Works," National Park Service (www.nps.gov/nr/travel/richmond/Tredegar.html).
17. *Fayetteville Weekly Observer*, October 21, 1861.
18. Pinkerton, *Spy of the Rebellion*, pp. 401–02.
19. Ibid.
20. Ibid.
21. Winkler, *Stealing Secrets*, pp. 89–93; Pinkerton, *Spy of the Rebellion*, pp. 314–15.
22. Ibid.
23. Ibid.
24. *Fayetteville Weekly Observer*, March 31, 1862.
25. Ibid.
26. Ibid.
27. Ibid.
28. Ibid.
29. Ibid.
30. Ibid.
31. Ibid.
32. Winkler, *Stealing Secrets*, pp. 297–98.
33. Ibid.
34. *Times-Picayune*, June 19, 1861.
35. *Emporia Weekly News*, October 5, 1861; *New York Tribune*, August 24, 1861.
36. Winkler, *Stealing Secrets*, pp. 297–98.
37. Winkler, *Stealing Secrets*, pp. 297–98; "Gideon Welles' View of War," HistoryNet (www.historynet.com/gideon-welles-view-of-war.htm).
38. Ibid.
39. Ibid.
40. Winkler, *Stealing Secrets*, pp. 297–98.
41. Silverstone, *Civil War Navies, 1855–1883*, pp. 113–15.
42. *Weekly Sun*, March 15, 1862.
43. Ibid.
44. Ibid.

45. Ibid.
46. Ibid.
47. Ibid.
48. *Indianapolis Indiana State Sentinel*, March 17, 1862.
49. Ibid.
50. Ibid.
51. Ibid.
52. Ibid.
53. Ibid.
54. Winkler, *Stealing Secrets*, pp. 89–93; "African American Women Spies," Civil War Women (civilwarwomenblog.com/african-american-women-spies/).

CHAPTER EIGHT

OPERATIVE ELIZABETH VAN LEW

SOUTHERN BELLE ELIZABETH VAN LEW STARED SADLY OUT THE WIN-dow of the hospital at the Libby Prison near Richmond, Virginia, at the current of disheveled, emaciated Union soldiers milling about a small, barren enclosure. The scene inside the facility was equally as distressing. Beds, almost touching one another, were crowded together and filled with sick and dying patients. Diarrhea, dysentery, scurvy, and gangrene were the diseases which had been the main course of the unfortunate inmates' existence for some time.[1]

The place was swarming with flies. Elizabeth, dressed in a modest skirt, blouse, and bonnet, fanned the insects away from the invalid to whom she had been reading. The ailing man caught her eye, forced a smile, and motioned to the book in her lap. She returned his smile, wearily passed her hand over her furrowed brow, and studied the opened page of the novel. Certain words and parts of words had been underlined in a seemingly random pattern. Read together in just the right order they revealed a message: the location of Confederate camps, the number of Rebel forces that were in a specific area, and what artillery they possessed.[2]

Federal prisoners in and out of the hospital furnished Elizabeth with information vital to the North's fight against the South. From the multi-windowed prison, they accurately estimated the strength of the passing troops and supply trains, the destination for which they were headed when they left town, and conversations overheard between surgeons, orderlies, and guards about planned attacks and casualties. Elizabeth dispatched the coded communication to Secret Service officials in Washington. The hospital and her prison ministries were a cloak to cover her real mission. Miss Van Lew was a spy.[3]

Born in Richmond, Virginia, in 1818, Elizabeth's family was wealthy and lived in a grand, three-and-a-half-story mansion. The attractive and amiable Miss Van Lew frequently attended lavish balls, garden parties, and elegant receptions. Great men and distinguished families were guests at the Van Lew home: General Ulysses S. Grant, songstress Jenny Lind, author Edgar Allan Poe, and John Adams, to name a few. Like other young ladies with her societal background, Elizabeth was educated at a prestigious school in Philadelphia. Although steeped in Southern tradition, neither Elizabeth nor her parents embraced the idea of owning slaves. They were abolitionists, influenced strongly by John Brown and the belief that the slave system could not be overthrown without force.[4]

Life for Northern sympathizers changed substantially when, shortly after the Civil War began, Richmond was made the capital of the Confederate states. Friends and neighbors in support of the South disapproved of Elizabeth and her family. The Van Lews had given freedom to the slaves they had and publicly denounced the ownership of any human being.[5]

While the ladies of Richmond sewed and knitted for the Confederacy, Elizabeth was writing letters to contacts in Washington, describing conditions in the South and providing information on troop numbers and their movements. In the beginning she sent letters through the mail, but just prior to the First Battle of Bull Run in July 1861, she used special messengers to deliver the dispatches.[6]

The First Battle of Bull Run was a Confederate victory. The Rebels took a number of Union soldiers as prisoners and marched them to Richmond, where they were interned at Libby Prison, a three-story brick warehouse on the waterfront of the James River. The sight of the many wounded and crippled soldiers crammed into such a small facility moved Elizabeth. She petitioned key Confederate military personnel to allow her to care for the inmates and bring the men books, food, and clothing. The provost marshal general of Richmond granted her permission to play

Portrait of Operative Elizabeth Van Lew COURTESY OF GRANGER HISTORICAL PICTURE ARCHIVE

nurse to the prisoners. Elizabeth was forty-three, and the Libby Prison was now her focus.[7]

Lieutenant David H. Todd (Mary Todd Lincoln's half-brother) was in command of the prison. Elizabeth won his favor with gifts of buttermilk and gingerbread. From the moment she gained access to the

117

prisoners, her dispatches to the government increased a hundredfold in accuracy and value.[8]

Southern sympathizers resented the kindness Elizabeth and her mother showed the Union prisoners. Threats were made against her and her family, and letters of criticism were submitted to newspapers. The July 29, 1861, edition of the *Richmond Examiner* contained an article condemning the two women who were attending the wounded Northerners:

> *Two ladies, mother and daughter, living on Church Hill, have lately attracted public notice by their assiduous attentions to the Yankee prisoners confined in the city. Whilst every true woman in this community has been busy making articles of comfort or necessity for our troops, or administering to the wants of the many hundreds of sick, who, from their homes, which they left to defend our soil, are fit subjects for our sympathy, these two women have been expending their opulent means in aiding and giving comfort to the miscreants who have invaded our sacred soil, bent on rape, murder, the desolation of our homes and sacred places, and the ruin and dishonor of our families.[9]*
>
> *Upon all pretexts of humanity! The largest human charity can find ample scope in kindness and attention to our own poor fellows who have been stricken down while battling for our country and our rights. The Yankee wounded have been put under charge of competent surgeons and provided with good nurses. This is more than they deserve and have any right to expect, and the course of these two females, in providing them with delicacies, stationery, and papers, cannot but be regarded as an evidence of sympathy amounting to an endorsing of the cause and conduct of these Northern vandals.[10]*

The public outcry and reports in the *Richmond Dispatch* and the *Richmond Examiner* newspapers prompted the Confederate Congress to pass a sequestration act in early August 1861. The act provided for confiscation of all Union "lands, tenements, goods, and chattels, rights and credits" and the transfer of debt obligation on the part of Confederate citizens; the act also applied to the Southerners who gave excessive aid and comfort to the Federals. Disapproving Richmond citizens suggested the Van Lews should be made to surrender all they had to the cause. "The threats, the scowls, the frowns of an infuriated community—who can write of them?" Elizabeth recalled about the time in her journal. "I have had brave men shake their fingers in my face and say terrible things. We had threats of being driven away, threats of fire, and threats of death."[11]

Despite the hatred and resentment of those around her, Elizabeth soldiered on. She maintained that her actions were those of a Christian woman, and that she was honor-bound to continue. Of course she was only referring to helping the prisoners and not necessarily the spying. In the spring of 1862, the Union Army was nearing Richmond, and she hoped they would overtake the city, but such was not the case. Still, she schemed, planned, and conferred secretly with the handful of Richmond Unionists. According to a *Harper's Monthly Magazine* report from June 1911, she disguised herself as a common farmhand in buckskin leggings, a one-piece skirt with waist of cotton, and a huge calico sunbonnet, and stole about the night on her secret mission. The article recounted her activities:

> *Through the blazing days of summer she worked the ill-stocked markets; bargained for the food sick men needed, paying for it with money that after a time she could ill afford to give. In the stark prisons and the fever-ridden wards; in the unfriendly crowds of the city streets, among those of the Confederate officers and officials themselves who still remained friendly despite the suspicions of the townspeople, she sought the recompense of her toil, the "information" that she required.[12]*

Elizabeth had several contacts in key locations in Richmond, one of whom was a woman employed as a waitress in the White House of the Confederacy. The former slave, Mary Elizabeth Bowser, spied on Confederate president Jefferson Davis and shared what she learned with Elizabeth, who in turn passed the intelligence along to Allan Pinkerton's Secret Service operatives. Elizabeth utilized a number of techniques to forward the information to Washington. Large baskets of eggs were often used, in which one egg was but a shell that contained a ciphered message; concealing a report in the sole of a shoe was also a favored

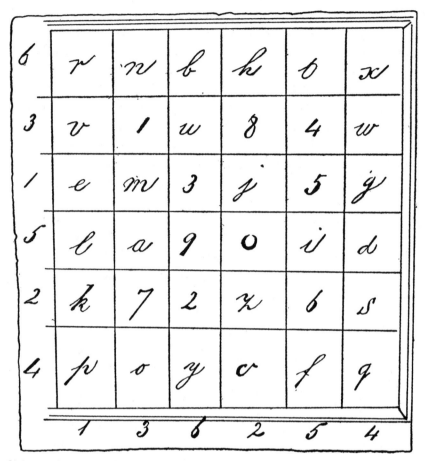

Cipher code used by Operative Elizabeth Van Lew COURTESY OF GRANGER HISTORICAL
PICTURE ARCHIVE

method. Elizabeth reconciled herself to the fact that she would eventually
be caught and tried for espionage. "The likelihood of such an occurrence
was inevitable," she noted in her journal. "From the commencement of
the war until its close, my life was in continual jeopardy."[13]

In December 1863, Elizabeth and the ring of spies she had assem-
bled were called upon by the government to help determine the number
and disposition of Rebel forces within Richmond. Secret Service operatives working directly with General Ulysses S. Grant desperately needed

the information in order to plan to overtake the city. No agent was able to enter Richmond. Elizabeth would be responsible for securing a way to secret the information out and into the hands of the general's aide. The messages were not only to be coded, but also written in colorless ink made visible only by coating the dispatch with milk. Elizabeth and the other Unionists she associated with divided their time between acquiring details about Southern troops and orchestrating an escape of Union officers held at Libby Prison.[14]

For several months, Elizabeth's colleagues, inmates within the prison, and agents who visited the men worked at digging a tunnel from the cellar of the prison to the outside world. Using chisels to dig and wooden spittoons to transport the dirt, more than a hundred men dug a sixty-foot-long pass to an open spot between two buildings beyond the gates of the prison. The majority of the men escaped. Several were hidden away in a secret room at the Van Lew mansion. When the time was right, Elizabeth helped the officers get to the Union lines.[15]

News of the "great escape" was reported in the February 11, 1864, edition of the *Richmond Examiner*:

> *One of those extraordinary escapades of prisoners of war, which have been very frequent on both sides, occurred at Libby Prison on Tuesday evening and at daylight yesterday morning. The discovery of the missing prisoners was first made at the daily morning count, when the number of prisoners fell alarmingly short. The roll was then restarted, as it always is when the count does not correspond with the number booked. The calling of the roll consumed nearly four hours.[16]*
>
> *At first it was suspicioned that the night sentinels had been bribed, and connived at the escape; and this suspicion received some credence from the statements of the Yankee officers who said the guards had passed them out by their posts. The officer of the guard and the sentinels on duty the night previous were accordingly placed under arrest by Major Turner, and after being searched for money or other evidence of their criminality.[17]*
>
> *In the meantime a thorough inspection of the basement of the prison, which slopes downward from Cary Street toward the river*

Elizabeth Van Lew's home in Richmond, Virginia, was a safe haven for Union prisoners of war. COURTESY OF THE LIBRARY OF CONGRESS

dock, began. This basement is very spacious and dark, and rarely opened except to receive commissary stores. . . . Once the dirt and stone was rolled away from the mouth of the sepulcher, revealed an avenue, which it was at once conjectured led to the outer world beyond. . . . So nicely was the distance gauged, that the inside of the enclosure was struck precisely, which hints strongly of outside measurement and assistance.[18]

All the labor must have been performed at night, and all traces of the work accomplished at night was closed up or cleared away before the morning light. The tunnel itself is a work of several months, being about three feet in diameter and at least sixty feet in length, with curvatures worked around rock. Upon the testimony afforded by the revelation of the tunnel, the imprisoned guards were at once released and restored to duty, the manner of the escape being too evident.[19]

Couriers were early dispatched in every direction, and the pickets double posted on all the roads and bridges. It is quite evident that the escaping prisoners have scattered and are traveling singularly or in pairs, or lying up in houses, or hiding places, provided for by the disloyal element to be found in and about Richmond, and will seek to steal off one by one in various guises other than that of the Yankee.[20]

Fifty-eight of the prisoners that escaped from Libby Prison safely reached the Union lines. Elizabeth wrote in her journal that the news of their successful arrival "gladdened her heart," but she was distressed that forty-eight of the escapees were recaptured. She was determined to secure the freedom of those recaptured officers and the thousands of others held and suffering. Confederate soldiers suspected Elizabeth had played a part in the Libby Prison incident, and were watching her every move. Undeterred, she continued to make regular visits to the Libby Prison as well as the Belle Isle Prison. She was able to charm her way inside both facilities using bribes and gifts.[21]

Five days prior to the prison breakout, Elizabeth had compiled the intelligence requested by General Grant's command, and she sent her first dispatch. The coded report noted that no attempt should be made to attack the Confederate capital and surrounding area with less than 30,000 cavalry, and between 10,000 and 15,000 infantry to support them. "Do not underrate their strength and desperation," Elizabeth wrote. "All women ought to be kept from passing from Baltimore to Richmond. They can do a great deal of harm. There is a Mrs. Graves who carried mail through to Portsmouth. Hope you watch her. The last time she brought mail into Portsmouth she came in a wagon selling corn."[22]

The spy's warning went unheeded. Major General Benjamin Butler, commander of the Union Department of Virginia and North Carolina, chose to strike the city with less than 6,000 troops, and the result was catastrophic. More than 330 Northern soldiers were killed or captured, and the loss served to bolster the diminishing spirits of the Southern people.[23]

Plans to burn Richmond to the ground after capturing Jefferson Davis and releasing the officers at Libby Prison were found on twenty-one-year-old Colonel Ulric Dahlgren. Dahlgren had lost his leg two months prior, and was traveling with his crutches strapped to his saddle and his artificial limb in his stirrup. Colonel Dahlgren and his small command were nearly wiped out in an ambush. In an account of the tragedy in her journal, Elizabeth wrote about the colonel's death and what followed:[24]

> *A coffin was made, and the body of Dahlgren placed in it and buried, where he was killed, at the fork of two roads, one leading from Stevensville and the other from Mantua Ferry. After a few days it was disinterred by order of the Confederate government, brought to Richmond, and lay for a time in a boxcar at the York River Railway station. It was buried, as the paper said, at eleven o'clock at night, no one knew where and no one should ever know.*[25]

Elizabeth did not mention in her reminiscences that it was her idea to steal Colonel Dahlgren's body; it was also her money used to purchase the metallic casket, which was used to hide Dahlgren's remains.[26]

According to the June 1911 edition of *Harper's Monthly Magazine*, Colonel Dahlgren's body was located by Mr. F. W. E. Lohmann and an unnamed slave. The unnamed slave was out walking late one evening when he saw Rebels burying a handicapped soldier. When he heard Mr. Lohmann was searching for the deceased, he took him to the plot where he'd been laid. Under cover of darkness, the two men unearthed the body and opened the coffin. Dahlgren was identified by the missing limb. The coffin was then loaded into a wagon and transported to an abandoned workshop. Mr. Lohmann sent for the metallic casket, and with the help of a handful of Union soldiers, transferred the colonel's remains to the casket.[27]

The *Harper's Monthly Magazine* article noted:

> *A few friends saw the body. Colonel Dahlgren's hair was very short, but all that could be spared was cut off and sent to his father. The coffin was then placed in the back of a wagon which was then filled with young peach trees packed as nurserymen packed them—the coffin, of course, being covered and concealed. A wagon driver named Mr.*

Rowley transported the brave Dahlgren through several pickets, one of which was then the strongest around Richmond. It was at this place the day before his death [where] Dahlgren fought for hours. Wary and vigilant were our pickets; if one had run his bayonet into the wagon only a few inches, death would have certainly been the reward of Rowley.[28]

Rowley was chosen well; Miss Van Lew's account shows him to have been a man of iron nerve and a consummate actor. At the picket post he listened without a quiver to the unexpected order that his wagon be searched; an inbound team drew up, and the picket, perceiving that Rowley gave no sign of being in a hurry, thoroughly searched it. The lieutenant of the post having reentered his tent, and one of the guard at that moment having recognized in Rowley a chance acquaintance, recalled to him their former meeting, there at once commenced a lively conversation. More wagons came, were searched, and went on. The lieutenant, looking out from his tent for an instant, gave orders each time to "search that man." The suspense must have been terrible; it seemed now that nothing would avert the discovery of the casket.[29]

"Your face is guarantee enough," the guard said to Rowley, in a low voice; "go on!" And so the body of Colonel Dahlgren resumed its journey to the farm of a German named Orrick. The grave was quickly dug and the coffin placed in it; two German women helped to fill it in and to plant over it one of the peach trees which had so successfully prevented discovery.[30]

Elizabeth's significant contribution to the Federal government during the Civil War was recognized by the Secret Service and General Grant after he became president.[31]

In 1864, the Union Army made another attempt to invade Richmond and overtake the city, and this time, they were successful. Residents in the Rebel capital fled the city when Federal troops invaded. The doomed Confederacy was in a panic to find horses to help their fighting men flee the area. Rather than see the North move in and seize their sacred domain, Southerners and Rebel soldiers set fire to houses, landmarks, and businesses. General Grant ordered men to find Elizabeth and help protect her home from the perils of the evacuation. When Union troops arrived at Elizabeth's house, they found her sitting in her living room on top of a stack of historic documents, her horse by her side. She wasn't going to let anyone take her mount.[32]

President Grant appointed Elizabeth Van Lew postmaster of Richmond, a position that paid $1,200 a year. The position proved to be a vital necessity for Elizabeth, as she had used all of her family's funds in her service for the Union and had no viable means of support. Her parents had passed away, and she was caring for her brother, a disabled, former soldier. "I live—and have lived for years—as entirely distinct from the citizens, as if I were plague-stricken," Elizabeth recalled in her journal, about her financial circumstances and reputation among Southern sympathizers. "Rarely, very rarely, is our doorbell ever rung by any but a pauper or those desiring my service. My mother was taken from me by death. We had not friends enough to be pallbearers."[33]

In 1877, Elizabeth was dismissed from her job as postmaster by President Rutherford B. Hayes. He succumbed to political opposition that was critical of a Federal spy and a woman being appointed to such a prestigious position. Life was difficult for Elizabeth after her job came to an end. According to the June 1911 edition of the *Harper's Monthly Magazine* (written several years after her death), "After her removal from office there followed years of distressing poverty and unavailing efforts to procure any sort of government appointment. Her salary during her time as postmaster had been spent chiefly on charities."

"I tell you truly and solemnly," she later wrote in her journal, "that I have suffered for necessary food. I have not one cent in the world. I honestly think that the government should see that I was sustained."[34]

Government officials, aware of the sacrifices Elizabeth had made during the Civil War, disagreed with President Hayes's decision to dismiss her. Many felt a sense of obligation to her. Officials saw to it that she was made a clerk at the Post Office Department in Washington. Sixty-five-year-old Elizabeth left her Richmond home to take the job, which turned out to be another heartbreaking experience. A vengeful supervisor made her work environment difficult. He berated her in front of her coworkers, demoted her rank, and reduced her pay. Elizabeth eventually resigned and returned to Virginia. She appealed to friends in the North to aid her in her time of need. Friends and relatives of the men Elizabeth had helped while serving at Libby Prison came to her rescue.[35]

Elizabeth Van Lew died on September 25, 1900, at her Richmond home, at three o'clock in the morning. The obituary that ran in the September 26, 1900, edition of the *New York Times* noted that she was eighty-three years old. "Miss Van Lew was the daughter of a wealthy Northern man," the article read, "who for a great many years was one of the principal hardware merchants of Richmond. She was a Union woman all during the war, and took no care to conceal the fact. She was constant in her ministrations to the prisoners confined in Libby Prison, and unknown to the Confederate authorities, was in frequent communication with General Grant's army."[36]

Among the items tucked into the pages of the journal Elizabeth maintained until the day she died was a torn piece of paper that summarized her life. "If I am entitled to the name of 'Spy' because I was in the Secret Service, I accept it willingly; but it will hereafter have in my mind a high and honorable signification. For my loyalty to my country I have two beautiful names—here I am called a 'Traitor'; farther North a 'Spy'—instead of the honored name of 'Faithful.'"[37]

Elizabeth was laid to rest at the Shockoe Hill Cemetery in Richmond, Virginia.[38]

NOTES

1. Varan, *Southern Lady, Yankee Spy: The True Story of Elizabeth Van Lew*, pp. 90–92; Ryan, *A Yankee Spy in Richmond*, pp. 2–5; Winkler, *Stealing Secrets*, pp. 54–56.
2. *Richmond Dispatch*, July 17, 1883; Varan, *Southern Lady, Yankee Spy*, pp. 90–92; Ryan, *A Yankee Spy in Richmond*, pp. 2–5; Winkler, *Stealing Secrets*, pp. 54–56.
3. Winkler, *Stealing Secrets*, pp. 57–59.
4. Ryan, *A Yankee Spy in Richmond*, pp. 25–28; Varan, *Southern Lady, Yankee Spy*, pp. 9–15.
5. Varan, *Southern Lady, Yankee Spy*, pp. 98–99.
6. *Richmond Dispatch*, July 17, 1883; Ryan, *A Yankee Spy in Richmond*, pp. 49–54.
7. Winkler, *Stealing Secrets*, pp. 54–57.
8. Varan, *Southern Lady, Yankee Spy*, pp. 56–60.
9. *Richmond Examiner*, July 29, 1861.
10. Ibid.

11. Ibid.
12. *Harper's Monthly Magazine*, June 11, 1911.
13. Winkler, *Stealing Secrets*, p. 80; Varan, *Southern Lady, Yankee Spy*, pp. 167–68.
14. Ryan, *A Yankee Spy in Richmond*, pp. 49–53.
15. Winkler, *Stealing Secrets*, pp. 66–69.
16. *Richmond Examiner*, February 11, 1864.
17. Ibid.
18. Ibid.
19. Ibid.
20. Ibid.
21. Winkler, *Stealing Secrets*, pp. 66–69; Ryan, A *Yankee Spy in Richmond*, pp. 58–60; *Richmond Whig*, February 13, 1864.
22. Ryan, *A Yankee Spy in Richmond*, pp. 59–61; Varan, *Southern Lady, Yankee Spy*, pp. 125–26.
23. Official Records, Ser. 1, Vol. XXXIII, January 30, 1864.
24. Official Records, Ser. 1, Vol. XXXIII, January 30, 1864; Varan, *Southern Lady, Yankee Spy*, pp. 141, 148–49.
25. Official Records, Ser. 1, Vol. XXXIII, January 30, 1864.
26. Winkler, *Stealing Secrets*, pp. 70–75.
27. *Harper's Monthly Magazine*, June 1911.
28. Ibid.
29. Ibid.
30. Ibid.
31. Winkler, *Stealing Secrets*, pp. 75–77; Varan, *Southern Lady, Yankee Spy*, pp. 188–89.
32. Ryan, *A Yankee Spy in Richmond*, pp. 107–09.
33. Varan, *Southern Lady, Yankee Spy*, pp. 218–39.
34. *Harper's Monthly Magazine*, June 1911.
35. Winkler, *Stealing Secrets*, pp. 84–86.
36. *New York Times*, September 26, 1900.
37. Winkler, *Stealing Secrets*, pp. 84–86; Varan, *Southern Lady, Yankee Spy*, pp. 218–39, 252–53.
38. Ibid.

Chapter Nine

OPERATIVE DR. MARY EDWARDS WALKER

Dr. Mary Edwards Walker caressed the heavy medal pinned on her lapel while staring at the letter in her hand. Frustrated and angry, she set the letter aside, then turned her attention to the document on the table next to her:

Medal of Honor
Dr. Mary Edwards Walker
November 11, 1865
Walker, Dr. Mary E.
Rank and organization:
Contract Acting Assistant Surgeon (civilian), US Army
Places and dates:
Battle of Bull Run, July 21, 1861;
Patent Office Hospital, Washington, DC, October 1861;
Chattanooga, Tennessee, following Battle of Chickamauga, September 1863;
Prisoner of War, April 10, 1864–August 12, 1864, Richmond, Virginia;
Battle of Atlanta, September 1864.
Entered service at:
Louisville, Kentucky
Born:

26 November 1832, Oswego County, New York
Citation:
Whereas it appears from official reports that Dr. Mary E. Walker, a graduate of medicine, "has rendered valuable service to the Government and her efforts have been earnest and untiring in a variety of ways," and that she was assigned to duty and served as an assistant surgeon in charge of female prisoners at Louisville, Kentucky, upon the recommendation of Major Generals Sherman and Thomas, and faithfully served as contract surgeon in the service of the United States, and has devoted herself with much patriotic zeal to the sick and wounded soldiers, both in the field and hospitals, to the detriment of her own health, and has also endured hardships as a prisoner of war four months in a Southern prison while acting as contract surgeon; and
Whereas by reason of her not being a commissioned officer in the military service, a brevet or honorary rank cannot, under existing laws, be conferred upon her; and
Whereas in the opinion of the President an honorable recognition of her services and sufferings should be made:
It is ordered, that a testimonial thereof shall be hereby made and given to the said Dr. Mary E. Walker, and that the usual medal of honor for meritorious services be given her.
Given under my hand in the city of Washington, DC, this 11th day of November, AD 1865.[1]

Now, after Dr. Walker had worn her medal proudly for fifty-two years, the US government had revoked the honor it had once bestowed upon her, and struck her name from the list of recipients. In mid-January of 1917, eighty-four-year-old Mary and 910 other recipients were notified that their medals were being rescinded because new regulations required "actual combat with an enemy . . . above and beyond the call of duty."[2] At the prompting and connivery of Secretary of War Edwin M. Stanton during the Civil War, it appears that the Federal government had abused its powers of issuance regarding the Twenty-Seventh Maine Volunteer Infantry Regiment when the War Department forwarded 864 medals to the commanding officer. With concern raised and a change in standards, a 1916 board of five army generals, led by Lieutenant General Nelson A. Miles, identified 911 awards for causes other than distinguished service. Mary E. Walker's and Buffalo Bill Cody's were among those identified. Even though her contribution had not been combat-related, Mary was infuriated by this great injustice—that her meritorious service was being disregarded by her government.

"They'll have to pry this from my cold, dead body," Mary fumed to herself. With firm and irrepressible determination, she kept the medal, wearing it until the day she died.[3]

Mary Edwards Walker knew controversy from the beginning, and was distinguished for her strength of mind and decision of character. Born in a farmhouse in Oswego Town, in Upstate New York, on November 26, 1832, her reform-oriented parents raised their children "in a progressive manner that was revolutionary for the time." Alvah and Vesta (Whitcomb) Walker's "nontraditional parenting nurtured Mary's spirit of independence and sense of justice, [which] she actively demonstrated throughout her life."[4]

Mary excelled in school, spurred on by her family's emphasis on and esteem for education, their focus on books, and the eventual founding of a school on their own property. In December of 1853, Mary attended one of the few medical institutions admitting females in those days, Syracuse Medical College. She graduated with honors in 1855, when she was awarded her Doctor of Medicine degree—one of only a handful of women in the United States to achieve this goal at the time. Although the degree gave her the right to practice medicine and surgery, it didn't guarantee that she'd have a successful practice.[5]

After graduation, Mary married a fellow student named Albert Miller, and they established a joint practice in Rome, New York. The marriage was troubled from the beginning, and the couple divorced shortly before the smoke cleared at Fort Sumter, signaling the start of the Civil War. Aware that there was a great need for physicians to serve in the military, Mary enthusiastically and confidently marched directly to the War Department in the City of Washington, requesting a surgeon's appointment of then secretary of war, Simon Cameron. Despite a shortage of medical personnel, facilities, and supplies, Cameron and the military were no more willing to accept a woman physician than was regular society.

The determined doctor was undaunted by her country's rejection.[6]

The unprepared capital city had been inundated with approximately 250,000 volunteers responding to Lincoln's "all call" to suppress the Confederacy. Now, it had been further besieged by masses of wounded and demoralized Union soldiers after their defeat at the First Battle of Bull Run / Manassas. In October 1861, Dr. Walker trudged along the overwhelmed, congested streets, visiting the relief hospitals. Mary's services were quickly accepted at the Indiana Hospital, commonly known as the Patent Office Hospital, because of its occupancy of the incomplete building's top floor.[7]

While at Indiana Hospital, Dr. Walker began what would become her war-long fight for a commission as a military surgeon with the medical department of the Union Army, even directly petitioning the surgeon general and assistant surgeon general. Despite not being on the payroll, Mary continued to render aid to wounded masses that poured into the city, acting as a volunteer assistant surgeon without the title.[8]

Mary was generous and kind to everyone with whom she came in contact at the hospital, and she met a number of influential people during her time at the facility. She was introduced to governors, congressmen, and national leaders, and was not shy about calling on them for help. Because of her positive presence, care, and concern, many of the soldiers' families needing assistance wrote directly to her. She was known as a person who would go above and beyond to lend a hand. Dr. Walker's reputation for tenderness and honesty spread.[9]

It was during her time at Indiana Hospital that she began accompanying patients to their homes, including several trips to Virginia. Traveling in this capacity gave Mary her first experience of seeing the South.[10]

Soon after Lincoln's first inauguration, Allan Pinkerton responded to the newly elected president's summons of April 28, 1861, where he presented his ideas of a secret intelligence service to Lincoln's new Cabinet in a private meeting in May. Unimpressed, the Cabinet adjourned with nothing accomplished.

On April 23, 1861, days before Lincoln's summons of Pinkerton, George B. McClellan had been commissioned a major general in command of the Ohio militia volunteers. The same day Pinkerton was presenting his notions to the executive Cabinet, McClellan "re-entered federal service as commander of the Department of the Ohio, responsible for the defense of the states of Ohio, Indiana, Illinois, and, later, western Pennsylvania, western Virginia, and Missouri." He was commissioned a major general in the regular army on May 14.[11]

On July 26, 1861, Major General George B. McClellan reached Washington and was appointed commander of the Military Division of the Potomac, the main Union force responsible for the capital's defense. After Virginia military units were consolidated into his department on August 20, McClellan formed the Army of the Potomac, he being its first commander.[12] Author Jay Bonansinga, of *Pinkerton's War: The Civil War's Greatest Spy and the Birth of the U.S. Secret Service*, states that McClellan "shared Pinkerton's pioneering vision for clandestine intelligence gathering." McClellan communicated with Pinkerton, writing: "Have heard of your achievement in protecting the President [*sic*] and would appreciate your coming to see me in Cincinnati. Observe caution. If you telegraph me, be sure to use only your first name. Let no one know your plans."[13]

Pinkerton gladly accepted the post of major, heading McClellan's "Secret Service," and overseeing all intelligence gathering throughout the western theater. As E. J. Allen, he assumed the role of a gentleman from Augusta, Georgia, traveling the backwaters on horseback and infiltrating troubled border areas.[14]

As early as September 1862, Dr. Walker had written to the secretary of war:

> *I again offer my services to my country. . . . I refer to my being sent to Richmond under a "flag of truce" for the relief of our sick soldiers and then use the style ([of double communication in writing their necessities]) that I invented, to give you information as [to] their forces and plans and any important information. No one knows what the style of writing is, except Hon. Mssrs. Cameron Seward and Mr. Allen of the "Secret Service". . . . Any "secret service" that your Hon. Body may wish performed will find in me one eminently fitted to do it.[15]*

Mary's own words, as well as her reference to Mr. Allen, clearly indicate that her intent was to subtly elicit and gather intelligence regarding Confederate military forces' locations and strengths, while portraying herself and performing her duties as a physician within the enemy's countryside. Sharon M. Harris, in her *Dr. Mary Walker: An American Radical, 1832–1919*, contends that the idea "the detective [Pinkerton] would have sought to engage Mary in the corps of his Secret Service is plausible."[16] The only response Mary received from this offer was said to have been written with careful words. It simply stated that her request for "employment in Secret Service" had been referred to Major General Henry Wager Halleck, the army's general in chief.[17]

Learning about the devastation resulting from the Battle of Antietam (September 17, 1862), and knowing that she would not receive a commission from the War Department, Dr. Walker headed straight for where she knew the need was greatest: the encampment near Warrenton, which held 120,000 men.[18] Presenting herself at the Virginia headquarters of Major General Ambrose Burnside, Mary was taken on as a field surgeon.

Back in the Federal capital city, by the time President Lincoln's Emancipation Proclamation took effect (signed, with finalized issuance) on January 1, 1863, Dr. Walker was becoming known as a political force in Washington, even joining President Lincoln at the Sixth Street Wharf as the Confederate prisoners of Chancellorsville arrived, and attending the annual Democratic receptions for the remainder of her life.

Almost one year after working with Burnside at Warrenton, Walker volunteered at the Chattanooga battlefield hospital in Tennessee, tending the masses of wounded soldiers after the Battle of Chickamauga, and meeting General George H. Thomas, who would prove to be an invaluable contact. Still wanting an official appointment to go to the battlefront, Mary devised and presented a plan to Secretary of War Stanton. Three days before Thomas was appointed commander of the Army of the Cumberland, on November 2, 1863, Mary wrote Stanton an unprecedented proposal: She wanted to establish a regiment of her own, named "Walker's U.S. Patriots," in which she would act as first assistant surgeon.[19] Mary appealed directly to Lincoln in January 1864 after receiving Stanton's rejection; he, too, denied her offer.

Needing a replacement assistant surgeon, General George H. Thomas recollected his own observations of Dr. Walker's skills, demonstrated during the Chickamauga Campaign, and wielded his authority as commander of the Army of the Cumberland. He intervened on Mary's behalf, and assigned Dr. Walker as the Fifty-Second Ohio Volunteers' civilian contract surgeon on March 14, 1864. Special Order No. 8 instructed her to "report without delay to Colonel Dan McCook."[20]

As directed, Dr. Walker reported to Gordon's Mills in northern Georgia, across the state line from Chattanooga. By the time Dr. Walker arrived at Gordon's Mills, most of the severe cases had been transported. It is while she was there that Colonel McCook suggested to Mary that she extend herself beyond the Union lines, to "render aid" to those needing medical (and dental) attention in the war-torn region around the Georgia-Tennessee border. Harris writes, "But her assignment there may have been for reasons beyond her medical skills." In her book *A Woman of Honor: Dr. Mary E. Walker and the Civil War*, Mercedes Graf adds, "There is some disagreement as to the nature of Walker's work in the countryside the winter of 1864. It was rumored that she had submitted a plan that involved her 'spying' for the Union while she acted as a contract surgeon. Since she often went deep into enemy territory to assist civilians with their medical problems, she had the perfect cover for such an activity."[21]

Although there are varied opinions among historians regarding Dr. Walker's spy status, Reverend Nixon B. Stewart, regimental historian of the Fifty-Second, documented, "How she got her commission 'no one seemed to know.' . . . [She] provided little in the way of medical services to . . . men of the 52nd. . . . It seems that she never was carried on the rolls, nor do we find her name on the Roster of Ohio soldiers. . . . She began to practice in her profession among the citizens. . . . Every day she would pass out of the picket line. . . . All this time many of the boys believed her to be a spy."[22]

According to the book *Healers and Achievers: Physicians Who Excelled in Other Fields and the Times in Which They Lived*, author Raphael S.

Bloch asserts that General George H. Thomas, commander of the Army of the Cumberland, confirmed Dr. Walker's efforts as a Civil War spy in writing years after the fact: "She desired to be sent to the 52nd [*sic*] Ohio as Acting Assistant Surgeon, so that she might get through our lines and get information of the enemy."[23] Harris further substantiates when she writes, "In 1865 the judge advocate general [Joseph Holt] revealed that 'at one time [she] gained information that led General Sherman to so modify his strategic operations as to save himself from a serious reverse and obtain success where defeat before seemed to be inevitable.'"[24]

Dr. Mary Walker was the most honored operative in Allan Pinkerton's Secret Service. COURTESY OF THE LIBRARY OF CONGRESS

Historians assert that Walker's request for a pension increase in the late 1870s was denied due to her services as a spy. Bloch continues the case by saying,

A decade after the war ended, one government agency was more forthcoming about her espionage. When in 1876 Mary petitioned the Federal Pension Office for a pension increase based on her contract surgeon service, the request was denied. The commissioner wrote, "Your appointment as contract surgeon was made for the purpose, not of performing duties pertaining to such office, but that you might be captured by the enemy to enable you to obtain information concerning their military affairs; in other words, you were to act in the role of a spy for the United States military authorities."

The statement leaves little room for doubt about his view of her mission. It also suggests that her capture by the Confederacy was planned, to facilitate her surveillance of the enemy.[25]

Argues Bloch: "President Johnson's order on November 11, 1865, awarding Walker the Medal of Honor, also hints that she served as a spy: '. . . Much of the service rendered by her to the Government could not have been accomplished by a man.'"[26]

Even Senate Report No. 237 of the 46th Congress, 2d Session, dated February 9, 1880, implies that among the services rendered by Dr. Walker was that of spying. Within the report, it reads:

The petitioner [Walker, who was petitioning for her pension] was assigned to duty as hospital nurse, March 12, 1864. . . . It appears that while acting in this capacity she wandered outside of the lines, and was taken prisoner, in accordance with a preconcerted arrangement entered into between her and the Federal officers, the petitioner thinking that she might obtain information while in the hands of the enemy which would be of value to the Federal officers.[27]

On April 10, 1864, while on an "expedition" and returning to Gordon's Mills, where she had been many times before, the doctor reportedly took a wrong road, encountering enemy pickets commanded

by General Daniel Harvey Hill. Suddenly finding herself a prisoner
of war, she was arrested and taken into Confederate custody less than
one month after her assignment to the Fifty-Second.[28]

Harris states, "Five days after Mary's capture, General Ulysses S. Grant ordered all women to leave Union battlefield areas. Many women and military leaders ignored the command, but what few knew was that Grant probably feared the exposure of the military's use of a woman spy."[29] The new prisoner of war was transported to General Joseph E. Johnston's headquarters at Dalton, Georgia, on April 12, 1864.

After recovering from major injuries sustained at the Battle of Seven Pines (May 31–June 1, 1862), Johnston was somewhat demoted and given command of the Western Department of the Confederacy, mostly an administrative post. According to Bloch, "During the Confederate occupation of Dalton, in the winter of 1863–1864, General Joseph E. Johnston and his staff officers were entertained in the Blunt house [home of Cherokee missionary Ainsworth Emery Blunt and wife Elizabeth]. While held there [Johnston's headquarters] for a week, [Dr. Walker] consented to treat some sick Southern soldiers." One of those may have been the general himself, because in early April, Johnston was laid up again with lingering problems from his wound. Now he was forced to contend with Dr. Mary E. Walker. After being held for several days, Walker was transported by rail some 700 miles to Castle Thunder Prison in Richmond, Virginia.[30]

Seized by the Confederate government for military purposes, Castle Thunder was in actuality three separate, large, old redbrick tobacco warehouses. Many Castle Thunder prisoners were awaiting death sentences due to the nature of their crimes. By November 1862, the prison was less than one year old, and run by new commandant Captain George W. Alexander, who was developing his reputation for brutality after only one month; even by Southerners' standards it was considered fearsome. The reports of unnecessary brutality brought about a Confederate House of Representatives investigation in the spring of 1863, possibly close to the time of Mary's incarceration.[31]

Mary's arrival at Castle Thunder received lots of publicity from the area newspapers. Graf states, "Many Southerners, however, assumed that Walker had engaged in spying activities for her government. Why else would she have been arrested? Their speculations would have seemed justified if they had been privy to the statement made the following year by the Judge Advocate General [Holt]." She continues by saying, "Nevertheless, she [Walker] had every intention of being a spy if the opportunity presented itself. A telegram from Army Headquarters substantiates this."

She then goes on to report Thomas's aforementioned letter. Furthering her case, Graf states, "A terse reply to Thomas from E. D. Townsend, Assistant Adjutant General, strongly suggests that Walker had been engaged in trying to gather information from the enemy as she rode about the countryside: 'Telegram received. Is there anything due the woman, and if so, what amount for secret service or other services. The object is to give her some funds in her need if anything is due.'" General Thomas responded to Townsend, "Her services have no doubt been valuable to the Government, and her efforts have been earnest and untiring and have been exerted in a variety of ways."[32]

Dr. Walker was never charged as a spy. After four months of imprisonment, she was exchanged on August 12, 1864, as a surgeon for a Southern surgeon with the rank of major. In the subsequent years, she would apply for a pension due to the effects of imprisonment rendering her unable to perform as a surgeon, and would continue to press for her commission, even writing General Sherman, stating that she had "acted in various capacities."[33] The commission she so desperately wanted and deserved continued to elude her for her remaining days. Relieved of duty on May 25, 1865, Mary and the army parted ways. Her service officially ended June 15, 1865.

After having been petitioned by Dr. Walker's many supporters, President Andrew Johnson was still unable to grant her request for a commission. However, driven by his belief that she deserved commendation of some kind, Johnson persisted until he found that Congress had passed an act in 1862 which allowed the US president, at his sole discretion, to award the Medal of Honor to an individual showing "unusual gallantry in action." In November of 1865, Mary received notification that President Johnson had signed the presidential order awarding her the Medal of Honor, making her the only woman to receive the country's highest military honor. It immediately became her most prized possession, and she wore it every day for the remainder of her life.[34]

Dr. Mary Edwards Walker died on February 21, 1919, at the age of eighty-seven, and was buried in the family plot at Rural Cemetery in Oswego, New York.[35]

NOTES

1. "Mary Edwards Walker," About North Georgia (www.aboutnorthgeorgia.com/ang/Mary_Edwards_Walker); "Mary Edwards Walker," American Civil War.com (americancivilwar.com/women/mary_edwards_walker.html).

2. "History," Congressional Medal of Honor Society (www.cmohs.org/medal-history.php).

3. "Dr. Mary E. Walker," Association of the United States Army (www.ausa.org/dr-mary-e-walker); "Mary Edwards Walker, Civil War Doctor," St. Lawrence Branch of AAUW (stlawrence.aauw-nys.org/walker.htm).

4. St. Lawrence Branch of AAUW (stlawrence.aauw-nys.org/walker.htm).

5. Harris, *Dr. Mary Walker: An American Radical*, pp. 9–10; Graf, *A Woman of Honor: Dr. Mary E. Walker and the Civil War*, pp. 44–46; Leonard, *Yankee Women: Gender Battles in the Civil War*, pp. 106–07.

6. Leonard, *Yankee Women: Gender Battles in the Civil War*, pp. 106–07.

7. Ibid.

8. Ibid.

9. Harris, *Dr. Mary Walker: An American Radical*, pp. 26–33.

10. Harris, *Dr. Mary Walker*, pp. 26–33; Graf, *A Woman of Honor*, p. 24.

11. Harris, *Dr. Mary Walker*, pp. 26–33.

12. Ibid.

13. Harris, *Dr. Mary Walker*, pp. 26–33; Bonansinga, *Pinkerton's War: The Civil War's Greatest Spy and the Birth of the US Secret Service*, pp. 139–40.

14. Bonansinga, *Pinkerton's War: The Civil War's Greatest Spy and the Birth of the US Secret Service*, pp. 139–40.

15. Ibid.

16. Graf, *A Woman of Honor*, p. 65.

17. Harris, *Dr. Mary Walker*, pp. 57–58.

18. Ibid., pp. 57–65.

19. Fitzgerald, *Mary Walker: Civil War Surgeon and Feminist*, p. 47; Graf, *A Woman of Honor*, p. 30; Leonard, *Yankee Women*, pp. 120–21.

20. Leonard, *Yankee Women*, pp. 120–21; Graf, *A Woman of Honor*, pp. 52–55.

21. Graf, *A Woman of Honor*, pp. 52–55; Harris, *Dr. Mary Walker*, pp. 55–57.

22. Harris, *Dr. Mary Walker*, pp. 55–57; Graf, *A Woman of Honor*, pp. 52–55.

23. Graf, *A Woman of Honor*, p. 58; Bloch, *Healers and Achievers: Physicians Who Excelled in Other Fields and the Times in Which They Lived*, p. 610.

24. Graf, *A Woman of Honor*, pp. 55–58; Harris, *Dr. Mary Walker*, pp. 55–57.

25. Bloch, *Healers and Achievers*, pp. 610–17; Graf, *A Woman of Honor*, pp. 66–68.

26. Bloch, *Healers and Achievers*, pp. 610–17.

27. Reports of Committees of the Senate of the United States for the First and Second Sessions, 1879–1880.

28. Graf, *A Woman of Honor*, p. 63; Bloch, *Healers and Achievers*, pp. 610–17.

29. Harris, *Dr. Mary Walker*, p. 58.

30. Bloch, *Healers and Achievers*, pp. 610–17.

31. Ibid.

32. Ibid.

33. Graf, *A Woman of Honor*, pp. 61–62.

34. Graf, *A Woman of Honor*, pp. 61–62; Harris, *Dr. Mary Walker*, pp. 73–74.

35. Harris, *Dr. Mary Walker*, pp. 73–74; Graf, *A Woman of Honor*, p. 79.

CHAPTER TEN

OPERATIVES
L. L. LUCILLE AND
MISS SEATON

THE NEWSPAPER AD THAT APPEARED IN PUBLICATIONS THROUGHOUT the city of Chicago in 1861 highlighted the talents of a fortune-teller named L. L. Lucille. The remarkable soothsayer whose descendants were from Egypt was making her first appearance in the Midwest, and invited residents to visit her at the Temple of Magic anytime between the hours of 10:00 a.m. and 1:00 p.m. "She will cast the horoscope of all callers," the advertisement boasted. "She will tell them the events of their past life and reveal what the future has in store. The Great Asiatic Sibyl proudly announced that she had cast the horoscope of all the crowned heads of Europe, Asia, Africa, and Oceania, and specialized in helping the sorrowful and afflicted. She will tell who loves you; who hates you; and who is trying to injure you. She will show you your future husband or wife." The fee for such services was $10.00.[1]

According to Allan Pinkerton, who had written the notice about Lucille, the trade of fortune-telling was unique at the time, and many people were attracted to the idea. Pinkerton described the mystic's place of business on Clark Street as nearly square, with a large mirror the shape of the doorway on one end. His description continued:

The wall and windows were draped with dark colored material that blocked any sunlight from getting through. There was a swinging lamp in all four corners of the room and one in the center. They were bronze and silver, with Oriental patterns, and they swung slowly around in a circle. Several charts, mystic symbols, and small gloves filled low shelves and a variety of tables. Near one of the tables was a small table upon which stood a peculiarly shaped retort, [vessel or chamber in which substances are distilled or decomposed by heat] and from this, issued pungent, aromatic incense.

It was into this mystic, perfumed setting that L. L. Lucille would greet enthusiastic patrons anxious to receive predictions about important aspects of their lives. Customers waited for the fortune-teller in a lounge area furnished with large easy chairs. At just the right time, the medium would slip into the room through the folds of a curtain at one side of a gigantic mirror. Kate Warne played the part of L. L. Lucille, and Pinkerton wrote in his case files that "he hardly knew her, so great was her disguise." Kate's face and hands were stained a clear olive, and instead of wearing her hair up as she usually did, it hung down in heavy masses to her waist. She wore a long dress made from rich fabric and trimmed with Oriental accents. She carried a small wand around which twined two serpents at the top. Her whole appearance was dignified and imposing. Pinkerton was confident that Kate would deliver a convincing performance and help apprehend the woman attempting to kill one of the agency's clients, Captain J. N. Sumner.

Captain J. N. Sumner visited Pinkerton at his Chicago office seeking help in late 1859. The fifty-year-old man owned a farm in Connecticut where he resided when he wasn't at sea. Pinkerton described him as a distinguished-looking gentleman with dark, curly hair. Captain Sumner had recently announced his intention to retire from his freight enterprise and was looking forward to relaxing on his land. He'd come to see Pinkerton because he believed someone close to him wanted him dead. He began by describing his upbringing and family. His parents were loving people who always encouraged his love for the sea. He left home when he was fifteen years old to be a sailor. His parents purchased a farm while he was away on his first sea voyage. The captain had one brother, who had died at an early age, and two sisters, Lucy and Annie. When

Allan Pinkerton ca. 1861 COURTESY OF THE LIBRARY OF CONGRESS

Sumner's mother and father passed away, the sisters cared for the farm. Lucy was twenty-two years old and married, and Annie was eighteen, rambunctious and wild. Captain Sumner loved each of his sisters, but favored Annie. He told Pinkerton that the fact Annie was the youngest and so beautiful made it easy to shower her with attention.

One year when the captain returned home from his travels, he brought with him a shipmate named Henry Thayer. He introduced Annie to Henry, and the two were instantly smitten. Henry would return to the farm with

Captain Sumner as often as he could. The couple eventually became engaged. While Henry was away on a voyage, Annie attended parties and dinners and basked in the attention paid to her by several stylish gentlemen. Captain Sumner told her that her behavior was worrisome, and advised her to curtail her flirtatious actions. Annie promised she would, but did the opposite. She'd accepted a beautiful amethyst ring from an admirer and refused to return it, even after Captain Sumner confronted her.

"If Henry knew of this," the captain warned Annie, "it would make trouble."

Annie flew into a rage. "Oh! So you are left here to watch me, are you?" she snapped. "Well, then just report to him [Henry] that I can get a better husband than he any day. I am not going to shut myself up like a nun in a convent for any man."

The relationship between brother and sister was strained after the incident. Captain Sumner was scheduled to take command of a new ship, and hoped the time apart would improve things between him and Annie.

When Captain Sumner returned home once again, Annie and Henry were married and living in New York. The family farm had been sold, and the funds from the sale divided equally between the three children. Henry and Annie appeared to be devoted to one another, and Henry was thriving in his career. He had been given command of a ship and was in high spirits. Captain Sumner believed that Annie was finally content with a life of domesticity, and wanted nothing more than to make her husband happy.

Nothing could have been further from the truth.

Annie began teaching music in Brooklyn and was earning a substantial amount of money. While Henry was out to sea, she had moved into a fashionable boardinghouse, was wearing stylish clothes, and frequented popular cafes and theaters with men who were anxious to escort her to any and every event. Again, Captain Sumner approached his sister to discuss the idea of leading a more "quiet life." Annie insisted that Henry approved of the way she was living, and to stay out of her affairs. Captain Sumner then turned to his sister Lucy in hopes that she would intervene.

A series of voyages kept him away from home, so several years passed before Captain Sumner saw either of his siblings again. Annie was thirty-two when he came home to New York on leave. "She was still teaching music," Captain Sumner informed Pinkerton. "She dressed as elegantly as ever and seemed very complacent and contented. . . . We strolled through the park for a time and then seated ourselves in a quiet spot." During their conversation, Annie broke the news to her brother that she and Henry had separated. She explained that Henry had become overly strict with her and demanded that she change. Heated words were exchanged and he walked out. Annie did not know where Henry was, nor had she heard from him since their argument.

When Captain Sumner pointed out to Annie that her careless actions were to blame for her marital troubles, she broke into tears. She confessed that the disagreement she and Henry had had was over the fact that she was keeping company with a particular gentleman. Henry was jealous and flew into a violent rage. Annie wanted her husband back but didn't know how to reach him, and didn't know if he would ever return.

"My next voyage was to the East Indies," Captain Sumner told Pinkerton. "I made inquiries about Henry at every port and asked the crew aboard every vessel I met at sea, but no one could tell me anything about Henry. It became evident that he had not only left the service of the company he worked for, but that he had disappeared from all localities where he was known."

Annie was happy to see her brother when he returned to her home after months of searching, but she wasn't alone. She was entertaining a man named Alonzo Pattmore. The two had been spending a great deal of time together. He was a politician and the owner of a hotel in Greenville, Ohio. He made frequent trips to the New York area where he had met Annie. He often accompanied her to the opera and various soirees. She had even traveled to see him in Ohio a time or two. Captain Sumner reported to Pinkerton that Pattmore was roughly forty-five years of age, well-mannered, and well-dressed. "His eyes were large and black but rather snaky," he added. Annie declined to listen to anything about Captain Sumner's quest to acquire information about Henry's whereabouts. She excused herself and went to the theater with Pattmore.

Appalled at her behavior, the captain determined he could not let his sister fall any further into what he perceived was a dangerous situation.

He was now fifty years old and set his sights on buying a farm and living the rest of his life in the country. He believed if he had a grand home he could persuade Annie to relocate with him. She would be away from the city and temptation and could possibly abandon her impetuous ways. A letter from Lucy assured the captain that Annie needed to be saved. Lucy had learned that Pattmore was married and had three children. Further involvement with Pattmore would only lead to scandal and ruin.

By the time Captain Sumner had settled his affairs, purchased the farm, and moved, Annie had accepted a teaching position at a school in Greenville and was reasonably certain she would never leave.

Captain Sumner wrote his sister to invite her to live with him. He promised he would provide for her every need and want, and that even when he was gone from the world he would provide generously for her care. Annie didn't want to leave in the middle of a school year, and she pleaded with him to visit with her in Ohio. The captain happily obliged. During his brief stay with his sister, Captain Sumner learned she was pregnant. He chastised her for her behavior but promised the sordid affair would be forgotten if she left Pattmore.

Annie became defensive and declared her undying love for the father of her child. She told her brother that she and Pattmore planned to marry as soon as his wife died. The fact that Mrs. Pattmore wasn't ill or hadn't been diagnosed with any terminal disease hadn't stopped them from talking about the woman as though she was soon to expire, or from making wedding arrangements.

Captain Sumner was livid. He argued with Annie and was finally able to persuade her that she had made a horrible mistake. She didn't want the humiliation of having a child outside of wedlock, and decided it would be best to end the relationship with Pattmore. The captain agreed and took his sister to his home near Chicago. She had an abortion in the city and spent time recovering at his house. She cried all the time and pleaded with her brother to find Pattmore and bring him to her. Against his better judgment the captain did as his sister asked.

While at Annie's bedside, Pattmore shared with her the news of his political aspirations and of his wife's sudden declining health. Pattmore predicted she would die soon. Annie made a speedy recovery and informed her brother that it was her deepest desire to marry Pattmore, and "enjoy the gay life in the nation's capital."

Captain Sumner reminded Annie about her husband Henry, but she refused to discuss him. She wanted only to discuss wills. She told her brother that everyone who owns property should have a will, and pressed him into having one drawn up. Captain Sumner had promised all he had to Annie, but she believed that promise needed to be in writing. As he was hopelessly dedicated to making certain Annie could maintain a quality life after he was gone, the captain complied with her wishes.

A few short days after having received the signed and notarized document, Annie asked if she could read it. Captain Sumner didn't refuse her request. "She seemed very much pleased at this," the captain shared with Pinkerton. "She said I was a dear, good brother, but she hoped it might be a long time before she should become heir to my property."

To reward her brother for his decision, Annie retrieved a bottle of ale from the cabinet and poured a glass for both of them. Thirty minutes after Captain Sumner drank the glass of ale, he became violently ill. The following morning he was feeling better physically, but couldn't shake the idea that his life was in danger. The hue in the opal ring he was wearing had changed slightly. The captain, a superstitious person, took the discoloration as an omen that he would soon die. Pinkerton could see nothing strange about the ring, but there was no mistaking that Captain Sumner was shaken.

"Mr. Pinkerton, I have positive knowledge that Annie has attempted to poison me three times," Captain Sumner confessed to the detective. "After putting poison in the ale, she afterwards gave me some in a cup of coffee, and, the third time, it was administered so secretly that I do not know when I took it. The third time, I nearly died, and it was only by the prompt attendance of a physician that I was saved. He said it was a metal poison which probably came off a copper kettle."

The captain bravely confronted his sister about his suspicions. She denied the charge at first, but after her brother told her about the change in his ring, she confessed. She, too, was incredibly superstitious. Annie begged her brother to forgive her. She was so remorseful and upset over what she'd done that she collapsed and had to be taken to her bed.

Before Annie fainted she told the captain that Pattmore had convinced her to try to kill him. "He reiterated to Annie that he would marry her when his wife was dead," Captain Sumner explained to Pinkerton. She wouldn't say if Pattmore was poisoning his wife. Captain Sumner needed Pinkerton's help to catch Pattmore and save his sister. Pinkerton agreed to take the unusual case.

It seemed unlikely to Pinkerton that Annie would say anything that might incriminate Pattmore, and Captain Sumner would object to any attempt to force her to do so. Although Annie had admitted to being weak, vain, and thoughtless, and that she'd been unfaithful to her husband, the captain would not allow her to be arrested for infidelity. Pinkerton's first order of business was to prevent any harm from coming to Mrs. Pattmore. Before Pinkerton could send an agent to protect Pattmore's wife, he received word that the woman had died.

Pinkerton was sure Annie knew more than she had told her brother about the attempts made on the captain's life, and what had caused Mrs. Pattmore's death. "She could tell all of Pattmore's secrets," Pinkerton wrote in the case file. "It would be easier to get the truth out of Annie than Pattmore," he surmised. Calling upon the information the captain had given him about Annie's superstitious streak, Pinkerton decided to take advantage of that trait to get her to confess. "I should entrust the case to one of my female detectives," he noted in his report. "She would be posted upon all points of Annie's history; she would be required to learn enough of astrology, clairvoyance, and mesmerism to pass for one of the genuine tribe."

The plan was for Annie to visit Kate, who would portray a fortune-teller. Kate would gain the woman's complete trust by revealing what she knew of her background. Annie would then tell all she knew about Pattmore as a means of helping Kate to read her future.

Pinkerton asked Captain Sumner to help him set the trap. With his assistance they could show Annie how vile a person Pattmore was, and the hold he had on her might loosen forever. The captain was to have a quarrel with Annie and, during the argument, burn the will he had drafted while she watched. He was to tell her that he had made a new will, leaving everything to Lucy. Pinkerton reasoned that Annie would be so furious with the captain's decision that she would try to harm him again.

In addition to assigning Kate to the case, Pinkerton used an operative Kate had trained, named Miss Seaton, to assist. Miss Seaton's job was to meet and befriend Annie and ultimately persuade her to visit fortune-teller L. L. Lucille. Miss Seaton made Annie's acquaintance at the post office after noticing Annie retrieving a letter from the postmaster. Annie was crumpling the letter in her hand when Miss Seaton introduced herself. She seemed upset by what she'd read. Word was sent to an operative named Miller, who was shadowing Pattmore, to pay attention to the mail Pattmore received, and from where it was sent. In a week's time, Pattmore received four letters from Chicago.

While Miss Seaton and Annie were becoming friends and the operative was keeping tabs on Pattmore, Pinkerton traveled to Greenville, Ohio, to speak with the coroner and persuade him to exhume Mrs. Pattmore's body to determine if she had been poisoned. With the help of two additional agents, Pinkerton was able to get Mrs. Pattmore's remains disinterred and arrange for an inquest.

Pattmore was nervous and annoyed when he heard the news about what was to be done to his deceased wife's remains. Miller followed the widower to the hotel he owned and witnessed him write out a quick note, place it in an envelope, and deliver it to the post office. Once Pattmore was out of sight, the agent pulled the letter from the drop box. The letter was addressed to Mrs. Annie Thayer in Chicago, Illinois. The agent opened and read the letter. In it, Pattmore warned Annie that a rumor had been started by his political enemies, that he had poisoned his wife. He wanted to let her know there was to be an inquest, and not to worry about what she might read in the newspapers. Pattmore signed the correspondence, "Ever Your Loving and Devoted Husband." The way Pattmore closed the letter made Pinkerton curious as to whether or not Pattmore and Annie had committed bigamy. Pinkerton decided to investigate that particular matter further.

Pattmore was uneasy and agitated the day the results of the examination of his late wife were revealed at the courthouse. According to the Pinkerton operative, Pattmore frequently tugged at his collar and fidgeted in his chair while waiting. He seemed to breathe a sigh of relief when the coroner and physician announced that Mrs. Pattmore's death was the result of dysentery. Pinkerton and his team were not satisfied that those conducting the autopsy had not been bribed by Pattmore. Unbeknownst to Pattmore, Pinkerton operatives then hired a doctor of their own to extract contents from Mrs. Pattmore's stomach and test it for poison.

Meanwhile, back in Chicago, Miss Seaton and Annie had become fast friends, but Annie still had not taken Miss Seaton into her confidence. Miss Seaton reported to Kate Warne that apart from two trips a day to the post office, Annie rarely went anywhere. Miss Seaton had been able to examine the contents of Annie's trunks, and had found numerous letters from Pattmore dating back several years. Kate made a mental note of everything Miss Seaton learned about Annie, from the woman's visits to the drugstore to her trouble sleeping. The information proved to be useful at the right time.

One afternoon Miss Seaton met Annie to go on a walk and found her looking over tarot cards spread out in front of her. She asked Annie what her fortune looked like, and Annie shared that she didn't really know how to read the cards, but did so want to know what the future held for her. Miss Seaton told her about L. L. Lucille and suggested they plan to stop at the soothsayer's studio.

When Miss Seaton and Annie arrived at the mystic's place of business, they found her standing beside a table under a peculiar light. Annie was taken aback at first, but when Lucille stretched out her hand and bid the woman to step forward, she became more at ease. Lucille directed Annie to a massive, cushioned chair and invited her to have a seat.

According to Pinkerton's notes on the case, Lucille took a seat opposite Annie.

"What would you like to know, my child?" Lucille asked. "State your errand quickly, as my time is short to unfold the mysteries of the future. Like the wandering Jew, I must forever advance upon my mission. What do you seek to know?"

Annie told her, "I've come to learn my future."

The performance Kate Warne delivered as L. L. Lucille was inspired. She asked leading questions that Annie would answer politely. Lucille then responded with lengthy soliloquies that included pertinent infor-mation about Annie's past, family, and close friends. The details, times, places, and circumstances were so exact that Annie was at a loss as to what to say. She sincerely believed that Lucille had acquired all the spe-cifics telepathically.

Lucille spoke of Annie's upbringing, parents, siblings, lover, and husband. She told Annie that the husband she thought was gone forever would soon return. If that prediction wasn't enough, she shared with the shaken woman what she knew about her troubles with an older woman. The woman she was referring to was Mrs. Pattmore.

"She constantly crosses paths with you," Lucille said, slipping in and out of a trance. "Why does she act so? What is the matter with her? She is often interfering with you, but is always followed by that man; he must be her enemy. See! A shadow falls over her! What does it mean? She fades away and vanishes. It must be death!"

"Death!" shrieked Annie as she fell backwards and fainted.

Miss Seaton helped to revive Annie, and escorted her out of the studio and toward home.

Annie was alarmed and frazzled. She was convinced that Lucille was the genuine article, and once she'd regained her composure, admitted to Miss Seaton how desperately she needed to return to the fortune-teller.

A few days prior to Annie's initial visit to Lucille's, Pinkerton's oper-atives in the Far East had tracked Henry Thayer to a shipping line he commanded in the South Seas. Henry had hoped that traveling would make him forget Annie, but it had not. Lucille would use this news to her advantage.

Miss Seaton and Annie's next visit with Lucille was just as emotional for the young woman as the first. Annie was seated across from Lucille, who looked her straight in the eye for several moments.

"There is some peculiar influence about you which prevents a clear reading of your future," Lucille explained to Annie. "Even your past, though much of it is easily determined, seems obscured by strange inconsistencies—not to say impossibilities. Some of the results were so startling as to make it necessary for me to refuse to reveal them until by a second test I can decide whether there was no mistake in the solution of certain calculations. Tonight, therefore, I shall do what rarely is necessary in reading the horoscope of ordinary humans—I must invoke the aid of my progenitor and master, Hermes."

According to Lucille, Hermes was an ancient king who could help her see Annie's future clearly. Annie was spellbound by Lucille and hung on every word she said. Lucille suddenly began to speak earnestly, with a faraway look in her eyes, as if she actually realized the presence of ghouls and goblins. Annie was terrified, but said nothing, and Lucille continued.

"There has been with you frequently, during your past years, a man some years older than yourself. He appears to have been a sailor and, though often away from you, he has always sought you out on his return. He loves you, and is undoubtedly your true friend; he is unmarried, yet he does not wish to make you his wife. He wears a peculiar ring which he obtained in the East Indies. He often consults this ring, and it informs him whether he is in danger, or the reverse. You do not love this sailor as well as he loves you, and he wishes to remove you from the other man. He does this to protect you.

"I cannot understand the actions of the woman whom I mentioned yesterday; I cannot tell whether she is living or dead. The man you love has been with her; he gave her something in a spoon, which she was forced to take. Ah! I see! It was a medicine, a white powder—and now begins the obscurity. Further on, I see that he visited you; you ran to meet him and plied him with caresses. If he were your husband, it would partly clear away the cloud. Is it so?"

"Yes," Annie replied, "he is my husband."

As the session continued, Annie wanted to know more.

Lucille conveyed to her that she couldn't go on unless Annie was completely forthcoming about everything. Any unconfessed deeds prevented the seer from seeing clearly. Annie agreed to hold nothing back. Lucille let the whereabouts of Henry be known, and questioned Annie about the other man she had married in his absence.

Annie was frightened and confessed to marrying Alonzo Pattmore in a private ceremony shortly after she became convinced that Henry was dead. Annie broke down and sobbed. "I have been very wicked, I know," she lamented.

According to Pinkerton, Annie returned a third time to see Lucille to learn what she needed to do to make amends for what she had done. She also wanted to know what she could do to ensure that she could be happy moving ahead.

Lucille explained that the only way to make things right and ensure a future filled with peace was to reunite with her "sailor husband" and abandon the notion of poisoning her brother. Annie burst into tears. She admitted to having the poison, but said now that she was going to use the poison to kill herself and not her brother. Annie was on the verge of revealing how Pattmore had killed his wife, but great sobs kept her from speaking.

"You are involved with someone who does not return the affections of a true husband," the sibyl continued, as she studied Annie's palm. "This man loves you only for selfish, sensual purposes; he will fondle you as a plaything for a few years, and then he will cast you off for a younger and more handsome rival, even as he has already put away his first wife for your sake. If you cannot give him up now, someday he will throw you aside or trample you underfoot. When he wearies of you, have you any doubt that he will murder you as he has already murdered his first wife?"

According to Pinkerton's writings, Lucille had spoken in a rapid, sibilant whisper, leaning forward so as to bring her eyes directly before Annie's face, and the effect was electric.

"Yes, the heartless villain murdered his wife by poisoning her. I can see it all as it occurred; it is a dreadful scene, yet I know that it must be true. A woman of middle age is lying in bed; she was evidently very handsome, but now she shows signs of a long illness. Your lover, her husband, enters, and he wishes to give her some medicine; but see, she motions him away, though she is unable to speak. She must know that he is going to poison her, yet she cannot help herself, and the nurse does not suspect his design. Now he has given her the poison, and she is writhing in an agony of pain. She is dead, and her husband is her murderer."

"Oh! For God's sake, spare me, spare me!" Annie exclaimed between her sobs.

Lucille explained that there was only one sure way to be saved, and that was for Annie to confess what she knew to a court of law. Lucille warned her of the sad fate that awaited her if she ever decided to see the "blackheart" again. She told Annie that she needed to tell the whole truth about her association with Alonzo Pattmore to a mysterious man who has secretly been following her. "He has great power, and if you follow his counsel, he can save you from harm," Lucille added.

When the session with the fortune-teller had ended, Annie left the office, still crying over what had transpired. Allan Pinkerton approached her on the street and introduced himself as the one who had been keeping an eye on her. Annie recognized him immediately as the one Lucille spoke of, and didn't hesitate to accompany him to his office. Through broken tears, Annie told Pinkerton the whole truth about her difficulties. Her story began with how happy she was when she and Henry had first married. She was lonely during his long voyages at sea, and it was during one of those lonely, vulnerable times that she had met Pattmore. Pattmore was lonely, too, and despondent over what to do about his wife. He felt he was wasting his life with a woman he didn't really love. Annie and Pattmore had an affair and she became pregnant. Shortly after the pregnancy was terminated, Pattmore convinced Annie that they needed to kill all those who stood in the way of their happiness. He would kill his wife, and Annie was to do away with her brother.

Annie was brokenhearted over her actions, and begged for forgiveness. Captain Sumner had no intention of pressing charges against his sister, but Pattmore was in danger of being charged with murder. Pinkerton released Annie into Captain Sumner's custody and promised all would go well for her if she stayed and devoted herself to change.

Physicians in Ohio found large traces of poison in Mrs. Pattmore's bowels. Pattmore was arrested, tried, and found guilty of murder. He was sentenced to ten years in prison.

Henry Thayer returned home to Annie, and they reconciled. The couple had two children and eventually moved to China, where Henry became a partner in a wealthy shipping firm. Captain Sumner kept Pinkerton apprised of his sister's remarkable reversal of fortune, and thanked the skilled operatives at the Pinkerton Detective Agency for the happy ending.[2]

The case of the murderer and the fortune-teller was the last known case Kate Warne worked. She died on January 28, 1868. Historians such as Daniel Stashower believed she succumbed to a "lingering illness." News of her passing was covered in newspapers from Pennsylvania to France. According to the March 21, 1868, edition of the *Philadelphia Press*, Kate was not a member of any church, but she was "buried with all the Christian graces." The article praised her strength and devotion to her job. "She was quick to perceive and prompt to act; she proved that females are useful in a sphere to which the wants of society have long been loath to assign them," the *Philadelphia Press* noted. "As she lived, so she died, a fearless, pure, and devoted woman."[3]

Kate is buried at the Graceland Cemetery in Chicago, alongside other Pinkerton operatives.

NOTES

1. Pinkerton, *The Detective and the Somnabulist; The Murderer and the Fortune Teller*, pp. 105–239.
2. Ibid.
3. *Philadelphia Press*, March 21, 1868; *Anglo Times*, March 28, 1868; *The Magnet, Agricultural, Commercial, and Family Gazette*, July 13, 1868.

BIBLIOGRAPHY

Newspapers

Alabama Daily Confederation, Montgomery, Alabama, June 22, 1860.
Anglo-American Times, London, England, March 26, 1868.
Bennington Banner, Bennington, Vermont, April 14, 1965.
Boston Post, Boston, Massachusetts, January 18, 1862.
———. May 25, 1869.
Boston Sunday Post, Boston, Massachusetts, October 31, 1915.
Brown County World, Hiawatha, Kansas, July 17, 1884.
Burlington Daily Hawk Eye, Burlington, Iowa, May 7, 1862.
Charlotte Democrat, Charlotte, North Carolina, October 18, 1864.
Chronicle-Telegram, Elyria, Ohio, January 3, 1982.
The Citizen, Macon, Georgia, 1859.
Clarksville Weekly Chronicle, Clarksville, Tennessee, July 19, 1861.
Clinton Republican, Wilmington, Ohio, April 8, 1869.
Colfax Gazette, Colfax, Washington, February 15, 1901.
Columbus Herald, Columbus, Indiana, November 23, 1883.
Daily Journal, Wilmington, North Carolina, September 19, 1861.
Daily Nashville Patriot, Nashville, Tennessee, October 25, 1861.
Decatur Morning Review, Decatur, Illinois, September 17, 1890.
Delaware County Daily Times, Primos, Pennsylvania, December 16, 1977.
Des Moines Register, Des Moines, Iowa, September 22, 1907.
———. September 22, 1951.
Detroit Free Press, Detroit, Michigan, February 23, 1868.
———. March 5, 1961.
Emporia Weekly News, Emporia, Kansas, October 5, 1861.
Fayetteville Semi-Weekly Observer, Fayetteville, North Carolina, February 28, 1861.
Fayetteville Weekly Observer, Fayetteville, North Carolina, March 4, 1861.
———. October 21, 1861.
———. March 31, 1862.
Gettysburg Times, Gettysburg, Pennsylvania, October 15, 2014.
Greenfield Daily Reporter, Greenfield, Indiana, February 12, 1936.
Harrisburg Telegraph, Harrisburg, Pennsylvania, January 9, 1871.
Hillsdale Daily News, Hillsdale, Michigan, February 10, 1972.
Idaho State Journal, Pocatello, Idaho, August 27, 1976.

Indianapolis Indiana State Sentinel, Indianapolis, Indiana, March 17, 1862.

Indiana State Guard, Indianapolis, Indiana, March 2, 1861.

Janesville Daily Gazette, Janesville, Wisconsin, September 6, 1856.

———. March 8, 1861.

———. September 25, 1861.

Jeffersonian Democrat, Chardon, Ohio, February 22, 1861.

Journal News, Hamilton, Ohio, December 14, 1975.

Lincoln Evening Journal, Lincoln, Nebraska, April 17, 1918.

Louisville Daily Courier, Louisville, Kansas, November 12, 1861.

The Magnet, Agricultural, Commercial, and Family Gazette, London, England, July 13, 1868.

McArthur Democrat, McArthur, Ohio, January 9, 1862.

McArthur Enquirer, Cincinnati, Ohio, March 19, 1868.

Memphis Daily Appeal, Memphis, Tennessee, April 13, 1861.

Milwaukee Sentinel, Milwaukee, Wisconsin, March 5, 1969.

Morning News, Belfast, Antrim, Northern Ireland, November 24, 1883.

National Republican, Washington, D.C., June 3, 1862.

National Tribune, Washington, D.C., November 8, 1900.

New Albany Daily Ledger, New Albany, Indiana, March 26, 1869.

Newbern Weekly Progress, Newbern, North Carolina, February 26, 1861.

New York Times, New York, New York, January 27, 1853.

———. June 4, 1856.

———. February 20, 1861.

———. February 25, 1861.

———. October 23, 1861.

———. September 26, 1900.

———. December 11, 1911.

New York Tribune, New York, New York, August 24, 1861.

Oakland Tribune, Oakland, California, April 3, 1975.

Oshkosh Daily Northwestern, Oshkosh, Wisconsin, October 6, 1883.

Philadelphia Press, Philadelphia, Pennsylvania, March 21, 1868.

Public Ledger, Philadelphia, Pennsylvania, July 4, 1860.

Richmond Dispatch, Richmond, Virginia, February 23, 1861.

———. October 8, 1864.

———. July 17, 1883.

Richmond Examiner, Richmond, Virginia, July 29, 1861.

———. February 2, 1864.

Richmond Whig, Richmond, Virginia, February 13, 1864.

St. Johnsbury Caledonian, St. Johnsbury, Vermont, July 17, 1884.

San Antonio Light, San Antonio, Texas, March 2, 1919.

Sedalia Democrat, Sedalia, Missouri, January 23, 1933.

Somerset Daily American, Somerset, Pennsylvania, February 6, 1971.

Stars and Stripes, Washington, DC, September 20, 1966.

Syracuse Herald, Syracuse, New York, October 7, 1911.

The Times, Clay Center, Kansas, November 8, 1883.
The Times, San Mateo, California, August 23, 1966.
Times-Picayune, New Orleans, Louisiana, June 19, 1861.
Tucson Daily Citizen, Tucson, Arizona, August 26, 1966.
Warren Mail, Warren, Pennsylvania, February 22, 1861.
————. February 29, 1868.
Washington Post, Washington, DC, February 16, 1913.
————. July 13, 1982.
Weekly Standard, Raleigh, North Carolina, October 2, 1861.
Weekly Sun, Hailey, Indiana, March 15, 1862.
Wilmington Journal, Wilmington, North Carolina, October 20, 1864.

Books

Bloch, Raphael S. *Healers and Achievers: Physicians Who Excelled in Other Fields and the Times in Which They Lived*. Bloomington, IN: Xlibris Corp., 2012.

Bonansinga, Jay. *Pinkerton's War: The Civil War's Greatest Spy and the Birth of the US Secret Service*. Guilford, CT: Lyons Press, 2012.

Chaffin, Tom. *The H. L. Hunley: The Secret Hope of the Confederacy*. New York: Hill & Wang, 2010.

Cooper, Edward. *Vinnie Ream: An American Sculptor*. Chicago: Chicago Review Press, 2009.

Cuthbert, Norma. *Lincoln and the Baltimore Plot*. San Marino, CA: Huntington Library, 1949.

Duffin, Allan T. *History in Blue: 160 Years of Women Police, Sheriffs, Detectives, and State Troopers*. New York: Kaplan Publishing, 2010.

Eggleston, Larry G. *Women in the Civil War: Extraordinary Stories of Spies, Nurses, Doctors, Crusaders, and Others*. Jefferson, NC: McFarland Publishing, 2009.

Emerson, Jason. *Giant in the Shadows: The Life of Robert T. Lincoln*. Carbondale: Southern Illinois University Press, 2012.

Fitzgerald, Stephanie. *Mary Walker: Civil War Surgeon and Feminist*. Tallahassee, FL: Compass Point Books, 2009.

Foster, G. Allen. *The Eyes and Ears of the Civil War*. Vancouver, BC, Canada: Criterion Books, 1964.

Frank, Lisa Tendrich. *Women in the American Civil War*, Vol. 1. Santa Barbara, CA: ABC-CLIO, 2007.

Graf, Mercedes. *A Woman of Honor: Dr. Mary E. Walker and the Civil War*. Scotland, United Kingdom: Thomas Nelson Publishing, 2001.

Harris, Sharon M. *Dr. Mary Walker: An American Radical, 1832–1919*. New Brunswick, NJ: Rutgers University Press, 2009.

Horan, James D. *The Pinkertons: The Detective Dynasty That Made History*. New York: Bonanza Books, 1967.

Jones, Wilmer. *Behind Enemy Lines: Civil War Spies, Raiders, and Guerrillas*. Baltimore: Taylor Trade Publishing, 2015.

Leonard, Elizabeth D. *Yankee Women: Gender Battles in the Civil War*. New York: W. W. Norton, 1995.

Moran, Frank. *The Eye That Never Sleeps: The History of the Pinkerton National Detective Agency*. Bloomington: Indiana University Press, 1982.

Morris, Thomas D. *Ordeal of the Union: Fruits of Manifest Destiny, 1847–1852*. New York: Collier Books, 1947.

Olmsted, Edwin. *Big Guns: Civil War Siege, Seacoast & Naval Cannon*. Chicago: Museum Restoration Service, 1997.

Pierce, Bessie L. *A History of Chicago: The Beginning of a City 1848–1871*. Chicago: University of Chicago Press, 2007.

Pinkerton, Allan. *The Expressman and the Detective*. Toronto, ON, Canada: Belford Brothers Publishing, 1877.

———. *History and Evidence of the Passage of Abraham Lincoln from Harrisburg to Washington on the 22nd–23rd February 1861* (private publication prepared by Allan Pinkerton, 1868).

———. *The Detective and the Somnambulist; The Murderer and the Fortune Teller*. Toronto, ON, Canada: Belford Brothers Publishing, 1877.

———. *Spy of the Rebellion*. Lincoln: University of Nebraska, 2011.

———. *Thirty Years a Detective*. Warwick, NY: 1500 Books, 2007.

Recko, Corey. *A Spy for the Union: The Life and Execution of Timothy Webster*. Jefferson, NC: McFarland Publishing, 2013.

Ross, Ishbel. *Rebel Rose: The Life of Rose O'Neal Greenhow, Confederate Spy*. Marietta, GA: Mockingbird Books, 1954.

Ryan, David D. *A Yankee Spy in Richmond: The Civil War Diary of "Crazy Bet" Van Lew*. Mechanicsburg, PA: Stackpole Books, 1996.

Silverstone, Paul H. *Civil War Navies: 1855–1883*. University Park, IL: US Navy Institute Press, 2000.

Stack-Sappey, Maureen. *Sculpting Lincoln: Letters from Vinnie*. Calkins Creek, Pennsylvania: Calkins Creek Publishing, 2007.

Stashower, Daniel. *The Secret Plot to Murder Lincoln Before the Civil War: The Hour of Peril*. New York: Minotaur Books, 2013.

Thomas, Emory M. *The Dogs of War*. London, England: Oxford University Press, 2011.

Trefousse, Han. *Historical Dictionary of Reconstruction*. Westport, CT: Greenwood Publishing, 1991.

Varan, Elizabeth R. *Southern Lady, Yankee Spy: The True Story of Elizabeth Van Lew, A Union Agent in the Heart of the Confederacy*. London, England: Oxford University Press, 2005.

Ward, Geoffrey, Rick Burns, and Ken Burns. *The Civil War*. New York: Alfred A. Knopf, Inc., 1990.

Wilson, William B. *History of the Pennsylvania Railroad Department of the Young Men's Christian Association of Pennsylvania*. London, England: Forgotten Books, 2016.

———. *History of the Philadelphia Railroad Company*. London, England: Forgotten Books, 1996.

Winkler, H. Donald. *Stealing Secrets: How a Few Daring Women Deceived Generals, Impacted Battles, and Altered the Course of the Civil War*. Naperville, IL: Cumberland House, 2010.

Zeinert, Karen. *Those Courageous Women of the Civil War*. Minneapolis: Millbrook Press, 1998.

Government Documents / Essays / Reports

Chemung County Historical Society. Correspondence with Chemung County Historical Society and Rachel Dworkin, September 29, 2015.

Chicago Historical Society. Correspondence from Mrs. Lewis Sawyer, Assistant Reference Librarian at Chicago Historical Society and Clark Wilcox, Elmira, New York, March 25, 1959.

Funk & Wagnalls New Encyclopedia Pamphlet, *Allan Pinkerton*, Volume 19, 1973.

Graceland Cemetery Company. Correspondence from L. B. Gaberdiel at Chicago Historical Society and Clark Wilcox, Elmira, New York, March 10, 1959.

Library of Congress Administration Files, 1857–1899, Re: Kate Warne; Boxes 23, 24, 25, 68–183.

Library of Congress Files: McClellan Papers, July 22, 1861, July 25, 1861.

Library of Congress Files, Re: Kate Warne, Assignments of Kate Warne, Superintendent of Female Department, Under Allan Pinkerton: (1) Murder of Mrs. Pattmore by her husband, Alonzo Pattmore at Greenville, Ohio.

———. (2) Theft of $50,000 from Adams Express Company at Montgomery, Alabama, by Nathan Maroney in 1858.

National Archives, Intelligence in the Civil War, CIA Publication, 1953.

———. Letter from T. P. Turner, commanding Libby Prison, requesting that Van Lew stop providing meals for certain prisoners, RG 109, Ch. 9, Vol. 199 ½, February 15, 1863.

———. President-Elect Abraham Lincoln's Address in Independence Hall, February 22, 1861.

Official Civil War Records, January 30, 1864–February 5, 1864, Series 1, Vol. XXXIII, Dispatch from Elizabeth Van Lew to General Benjamin Butler.

———. Libby Prison Report, 1866.

Reports of Committee of the Senate of the United States for the First and Second Session of the Forty-Sixth Congress, 1879–80. Washington, DC: Government Printing Office.

Senate Report, No. 237, 40th Congress, February 9, 1880.

Periodicals/Journals

American Weekly Magazine, New York, New York, February 11, 1951.

Ebony Magazine, Vol. 20, No. 4, Chicago, Illinois, February 1965.

———. Vol. 33, No. 12, Chicago, Illinois, October 1978.

Harper's Monthly Magazine, Vol. XXXVII, New York, New York, June 1868.

————.Vol. MCMXII New York, New York, June 1911.

McClure's Magazine, New York, New York, November 1894.

The Rail Splitter: A Journal for the Lincoln Collector, Vol. 6, New York, New York, Fall 2000.

Wall, Hannah. "Never to be Forgotten: The Tale of Women Spies During the Civil War," Undergraduate Research Journal at UCCS Department of History, University of Colorado, Colorado Springs, Vol. 2.1 (Spring 2009).

The Windsor Magazine, Vol. 7, London, England, 1898.

Websites

"African American Women Spies," Civil War Women (civilwarwomenblog.com/african -american-women-spies/).

"Black Dispatches: Black American Contributions to Union Intelligence during the Civil War," Central Intelligence Agency (www.cia.gov/library/center-for-the-study-of -intelligence/csi-publications/books-and-monographs/black-dispatches/).

"Civil War Submarine," American Civil War Story (www.americancivilwarstory.com/ civil-war-submarine.html).

"The Confederate Sequestration Act," Project Muse (muse.jhu.edu/article/205276).

"CSS *Virginia*," American Civil War Story (www.americancivilwarstory.com/tcwn/ civil_war/Navy_Ships/CSS_Virginia.html).

"Dr. Mary E. Walker," Association of the United States Army (www.ausa.org/dr-mary -e-walker).

"The Express Companies," Midcontinent.org (www.midcontinent.org/rollingstock/ dictionary/express_companies.htm).

"Gideon Welles' View of War," HistoryNet (www.historynet.com/gideon-welles-view -of-war.htm).

"History," Congressional Medal of Honor Society (www.cmohs.org/medal-history.php).

"A History of Women and Policing," National Center for Women and Policing (womenandpolicing.com/history/historytext.htm).

"Introducing Charles Rawn, His Journals, and Their Editors," The Rawn Journals 1830–1865 (dauphincountyhistory.org/backups/rawn/about/).

"Jane Maxwell Drysdale" (www.ancestry.com/genealogy/records/jane-maxwell -drysdale_45857219).

"Kate Warne and Women's Security Careers Today," Pinkerton (www.pinkerton.com/ blog/kate-warne-women-security-careers-today).

"Kate Warne, First Female Private Eye," Thomas Investigative Publications (www .pimall.com/nais/pivintage/katewarne.html).

"Kate Warne: The First 'Pink Lady,'" The Pinkerton Detective Series . . . EXTRA (www.emillerbooks.com/Kate_Warne_The_First_Pink_Lady.html).

"Kate Warne Never Sleeps," Remarkable Travels (remarkable-travels.blogspot.com/ 2013/08/kate-warne-never-sleeps.html).

"Kate Warne: Union Spy and First Female Private Investigator," Civil War Women (civilwarwomenblog.com/kate-warne).

"Mary Edwards Walker," About North Georgia (www.aboutnorthgeorgia.com/ang/
    Mary_Edwards_Walker).

"Mary Edwards Walker," American Civil War.com (americancivilwar.com/women/
    mary_edwards_walker.html).

"Mary Edwards Walker, Civil War Doctor," St. Lawrence Branch of AAUW
    (stlawrence.aauw-nys.org/walker.htm).

"Submarines in the Civil War," The Civil War (www.navyandmarine.org/ondeck/
    1862submarines.htm).

"Tredegar Iron Works," National Park Service (www.nps.gov/nr/travel/richmond/
    Tredegar.html).

Undersea Warfare Magazine, US Navy (www.public.navy.mil/subfor/underseawarfare
    magazine/Issues/PDF/USW_Spring_2007.pdf).

"US Secret Service History," Secret Service (www.secretservice.gov/about/history/
    events).

INDEX

ABOUT THE AUTHOR

Chris Enss is a *New York Times* best-selling author who has been writing about women of the Old West for more than a dozen years. She has penned more than thirty published books—including more than two dozen for TwoDot—many about some of the most famous names in history, film, and popular culture. Her book entitled *Object Matrimony: The Risky Business of Mail Order Matchmaking on the Western Frontier* won the Elmer Kelton Award for best nonfiction book of 2013. Enss's book *Sam Sixkiller: Frontier Cherokee Lawman* was named Outstanding Book on Oklahoma History by the Oklahoma Historical Society. She received the Spirit of the West Alive award, cosponsored by the *Wild West Gazette*, celebrating her efforts to keep the spirit of the Old West alive for future generations.

Enss is also a scriptwriter and comedienne who has written for television and film, and performed on cruise ships and onstage. She has worked with award-winning musicians, writers, directors, and producers, and as a screenwriter for Tricor Entertainment. And she's a licensed private detective.